Fordritishope

ISTORY OF A SHROPSHIRE PARISH

Hope Bowdler,
Ragdon and Chelmick

'Fordritishope' - Domesday name of Hope Bowdler

Cover - 'Hope Bowdler from Mount Flirt' September 1871
by R G Benson.

In writing this book, I have tried to produce an historical and social commentary of the Parish. Wherever possible I have recorded facts, but as much of my source material could not be cross-checked - being extracted from documents and record books made at the time by individuals - there may be some errors.

The extracts from letters, documents, day books etc., are verbatim and the reader will find some of the language and spelling different from today, but as they are true of life at the time, they have all been reprinted as written.

There is a risk when interpreting events or making certain assumptions that, once printed, they can be taken as facts. In much the same way the records of family names, dates of births, marriages and deaths were often difficult to decipher from the scant or illegible records. For any inaccuracies, I apologise.

Finally, I am most grateful to the many people who searched their memories and photograph albums, in particular Norman Jones and Peter Morgan. Also for the documentary material provided by the Local Studies and County Archives in Shrewsbury and the Public Record Office in London.

Alan Dakers
Ragdon, 1986

ISBN 0 9512250 0 6

Published by A Dakers, Ragdon, Church Stretton SY6 7EY.

Printed by Orphans Press Ltd., Leominster.

CONTENTS

INTRODUCTION

A 'hope' signifies a narrow valley between two hills and is of Celtic derivation.

Although Stone Age finds have been made in Shropshire, there is no evidence of any connected with Hope Bowdler. However, by the time the Romans arrived, the Iron Age Celts were already strongly established in this area and there is evidence of many clashes between Celts and Romans.

To the north of the Parish border lies the Celtic Hill Fort of Caer Caradoc, with the lines of the fortifications still clearly visible. There is an Iron Age road to the summit. It was at one time thought that this was the fort where Caractacus made his last stand and he was supposed to have sheltered in the small cave on the western slope. (Caradoc is the Celtic form of Caractacus). However, while this was not the case, Caer Caradoc did acquire its name from having been one of the military stations of Caractacus.

There is no doubt that the Romans had a troublesome time subdueing the Celtic population in the area. It was an area heavily occupied by military forces. There was a Roman station at Rushbury and the name 'Wall' for a large area between it and Hope Bowdler probably derives from Roman fortifications. There are remains of a Roman roadway and pack horse bridges in the area.

Celtic influence remained and some of the native population stayed on in spite of Roman and Anglo-Saxon occupations.

The Celtic pattern of settlement and agriculture of small individual plots has survived instead of the more usual open field system of feudal times. This scattered pattern of settlements as revealed in the Domesday Book is that of tiny hamlets. Within the Hope Bowdler parish this is illustrated by the two townships of Chelmick and Ragdon.

There is also the fact that the local geography played a large part in the retention of the Celtic mode, as a 'hope' gives only isolated pockets of fertile ground interspersed with moorland and hill areas. There was no suitable area large enough to form a communal open field so that, to a certain extent, the Celtic system was a matter of necessity. It is reasonable to assume that while the Celts remained, so Anglo-Saxons tended to infiltrate into this area, rather than overwhelm it.

Most of the place names and many dialect words are of Anglo-Saxon origin.

The Vikings attacked Shrewsbury and the Abbey at Much Wenlock, but there is no evidence of their ever reaching this area.

VILLAGE LIFE - 18th/19th Century

The Parish of Hope Bowdler in 1841 totalled some 1800 acres, with a rateable value of £672-3-6 and had 34 houses, of which four were uninhabited, with 184 men, women and children. The Parish was divided into three, with the township of Chelmick having 13 houses and 49 people in its 305 acres, and Ragdon just two houses and 23 people in its 339 acres. The village, as such, was Hope Bowdler with 19 houses and 112 inhabitants and it, together with all the 1180 acres of hill and farmland formed the Hope Bowdler Estate, except for the house of John Croxton the blacksmith, whose grandfather was given the title to the house and certain lands by William Lutwyche back in 1759 and two small houses belonging to the Widow Gough in 1819 and later to John Broom.

For at least the last two centuries the Hope Bowdler Estate had been owned by landlords who lived out of the area. The only exception was W. Cheney Hart who did live in the Manor House in the late 1700's until his death in 1819. Following his death, the Estate was bought by the Benson family who also owned the Ragleth Hill and many properties in Church Stretton. They, through their bailiff Thomas Mytton, were very stern landlords and with a member of the family installed as Vicar in the second half of the 19th century, their influence was very much felt by all. Woe betide anyone who did not go to Church, whatever their religion, or hung their washing out on a Sunday or let their dogs run loose on Bowdler Hill.

Hope Bowdler was never a very important or thriving community. Farming was, quite naturally, the main occupation with practically everybody being entirely dependent on it, either through working on the land or with the blacksmith and wheelwright. A few worked in the stone quarries.

There is no record of there ever being a shop until after 1900 when groceries and refreshments were sold from 'The Haven' for a while.

There was no Inn with an official name ever listed. However, in 1819 when the Estate was put up for auction on the death of W. C. Hart, reference 127 (the site of The Haven) was listed in the Sale catalogue as 'Public House, fold and garden'. The term 'Public House' was not used to indicate an Inn at that time, and it was more probably because it accommodated 'lodgers'. In 1880 Mr. Morris of Soudley recalled that there were twelve apprentices who slept in the big attic room. What is not recorded is to what trade they were apprenticed. However, around 1838, when various properties were inspected and commented upon for a Rev. Ratcliff (who appears to have been interested in buying some) there is a reference to 'Hope Bowdler Inn', adding "the custom of this house is but little". It does not appear again in any records and probably gave up. It must be remembered that all the larger houses and farms had brew houses and ale cellars, and most people brewed their own beer, so the demand would not have been very great. But this did not stop John Croxton applying for a licence in 1851 as 'Brewer and retailer of ale, beer, porter and cider. Also a dealer in tobacco in my dwelling house situated in Hope Bowdler.' The licence was not granted.

Beer was cheap (and strong) - tea and coffee were still luxuries - and it has been estimated that at that time one seventh of total income was spent on drink, and between one and two pints a day were drunk by every man, woman and child in the country. But it was as a social drink that it was abused. Fairs were notorious for their drunkenness, and the ale house was paid a visit daily. Hours of work were long, jobs were often hard and tedious, and drink offered the easiest route to escape. Where else could one find cheerful company when work was done? Houses were cold and draughty. Consumer goods were few and far between, and entertainment not easy to find. The ale house was the ruin of many.

Although one can say that people's wants were less, that they produced more in their gardens, bred pigs, caught rabbits, etc. it was still more than two miles to the nearest shop - in Church Stretton. This was either walked, both ways, or by cart or pony and trap. There was a charge to be paid at the Toll House at Hazler Gate until the latter part of the 1800's.

There were traders who brought round by horse and cart at least some of the day-to-day essentials, because there is, for instance, reference to butchers living at Soudley and in Chelmick Valley, and although they may have done a certain amount of travelling around selling meat, their main purpose as butchers was in killing and dressing meat for the local inhabitants. Bakers were not in evidence, as nearly every house had its own bread oven and home baking was normal practice.

Church Stretton itself was little more than a village in 1841, having a population of only 631 people over 16 years of age, a variety of shops, and no less than nine inns from which to choose - Crown, Talbot, Lion, Plough, Bucks Head, Kings Arms, Brittania, Queens Head and Raven. There were still more at All Stretton and Little Stretton.

On June 26th 1214 King John granted to Stretton the right to hold a market on Wednesdays and a Yearly Fair on the Feast of Assumption. This was changed by Edward III in 1342 when he gave Stretton to the Earl of Arundel and granted a weekly market on Thursdays and a Yearly Fair on the eve, the day and the morrow of the Exaltation of the Holy Cross. In 1609 a Market Charter was granted by James 1.

The weekly market and, in particular, the Annual Fair were important events in the local life. The Fair was the major event of the year and had the added importance of also being the Hiring Fair, when men, boys and girls were taken on for the following year's work on the farms and in the big houses.

There were two doctors in Church Stretton in the early 1800's. William Wilding who lived at 17 High Street, and with his son Richard and grandson William were doctors in the town for around 100 years. Charles Mott was the other one. Two example of the charges for attendance are:-

1845:	Charles Mott, Surgeon.	
	Three powders for a child	1s 6d
	A mixture & box of pills	4s 0d
	Three powders & a journey	4s 0d
	Extracting a tooth	1s 0d
		10s 6d
1853	April to October for Mrs. Croxton	
	(who died)	£5-15-6
	Also, Bill for the family 1846/7/8/9 & 1852	£3- 2-0

The cost of calling the doctor or the difficulties involved in going to see one meant that a lot of curing was done by old-fashioned remedies, and one could be found for nearly every ill. For example:-

In 1790: "To make teeth fall out without pain - take the powder of rats tail and rub the teeth you would have out, but take care you do not tuch the rest."

In 1850: to get rid of bugs - "The spirit of Tar is so powerful a poison to those nightly visitors that as soon as it comes in contact with one it instantly dies. It should be applied by means of a small painting brush to the joints and crevices or cracks in the bedsteads and also their places of retreat in the wainscot or wall."

For rheumatism - a very common complaint:-

Rheumatism cure: ¼ pound of Treacle
¼ ounce Sulphur
¼ ounce Gumguaigum
¼ ounce Nitric
¼ ounce Rhubarb
One teaspoonful to be taken at bedtime.

To a large extent villagers were self-sufficient in their requirements for food, growing their own vegetables, keeping and curing a pig, rabbiting, grinding corn and such groceries as they had to purchase from time to time were probably paid for at the time. Details of costs are, therefore, not easy to find, but the following examples from household accounts are interesting.

1786:	Clening my Coate		3s 0d
	Mending hose		1s 0d
	Honey		2s 0d
	Tea		5s 0d
	Tea		1s 9d
	Sugar		8d
	Tea		6d
	Repairing coat		15s 0d
	Hatt		1s 0d
	Tea & Sugar		1s 9½
	2 yds of cotton		2s 8d
	Buttons & silk		1s 2d
	Sugar		8d
1788	May 25 Five bushels of Malt	£1	1s 6d
	June 21 Three of malt & hops ½lb		18s 2d
	July 11 2 strike of malt & hops		11s 0d
1810	Oct 23 A bag of Barley of Mr Evans at 8s3d a bushel	£1	4s 9d
1812	Aug 4 I had a bushel of corne of Mr Haynes, Ragdon	£1	6s 0d
1829	One pound Sugar		7d
	Baisin		1s 1½
	Ground spice		5d
	Peck of flour		3s 4d
	Lump sugar		1s 0d
	Paid for letter		6d
	" " "		5d
1838	April 7 - bought of Mr Wilgate		
	1 lb of candles		7d
	Bread		6d
	"		5d
	Flower		4d
	Bread		3d
	Salt		3d
	½ a peck of flower		1s 10½
	500 of coal		6s 8½
			10s 8½
1825	Mar 12 - bought of Hadley Co., Canal Wharf, Shrewsbury		
	1 ton coal net		14s 2d
1832	Mar 25 - bought of Mr Richard Dodd		
	half a strike of flower		4s 6d
	Tea		4d
	Shuger		3d
	Spice		1d
			5s 2d

A strickle or strike was a measure by passing a rod across the top of a heaped vessel - half a strik = 2 pecks, therefore, one strik = 1 bushel.

1832	- bought of Mr Richard Dodd		
	April 8	1 oz of Tobacco	3d
	April 10	A peck & half flower	3s 4½
	April 12	1 oz of Tobacco	3d
	April 16	1 oz of Tobacco	3d
	April 17	Shuger	3d
	April 27	Tea 2d, Shuger 3d, Candles 1d	6d
	May 7	Currands 3d, Spice 1d, Tobacco 1½d	5½
			5s 4d

Thomas Griffiths was a butcher in the village, and the following account with him shows nearly one year's purchases by a family.

1810	Feb 8	a Loyne of Mutton 3½pd for 7d	2s	0½
	" 17	a for quarter of mutton 9½pd at 7½d	5s	11½
	" 28	30pd Beef 5½d	13s	9d
		a shin & Skurts	2s	0d
	Mar 6	30pd of Beef at 7d	17s	6d
		The Hart & Skurts	2s	6d
	April 7	A stricken of Beef 15pd at 6½	8s	1d
	" 21	a neck of veal 5½pd at 6½	2s	11¾
	June 7	a shoulder of veal 10pd at 5½	4s	7d
	Julu 20	Calf belly	1s	0d
	Aug 8	a quarter of Lamb 8pd at 7d	4s	8d
	Oct 5	Ribs of Beef 9pd at 7d	5s	3d
	Nove 4	12pd of Pork at 8½d	8s	6d

In addition to the people who lived and worked in the village, men and women were hired for work on an annual basis at the Hiring Fair held in Church Stretton each year on or about May 14th. An annual sum was agreed and, in addition, food and lodging were given. The farmers were, naturally, the biggest employers and the details in each of the Census Returns show many of these and their different tasks.

As is recorded elsewhere, the Croxton family were blacksmiths in the village in the 18th and 19th centuries, and some interesting details from the family notebooks on the subject of Hiring are:-

1855	May 14	I hired Thomas Yap for £8 8s 0d
	Oct 11	I hired William Robarts to serve me to Stretton Fair 14 May for £4 0s 0d
1856		I hired Tom Carter to serve me for one year £2 0s 0d (almost certainly a young boy)
1856		I hired Charles Smout 14th May to serve me for one year is time to be up 14th May 1857. To give or take a Month notice or a Month wages £7 7s 0d
1857	May 14	Hired Charles Smout to stop a Gain (again) for one year is time to be up 14 May 1858 for £8 8s 0d

1858	May 14 Hired Charles Smout to stop a Gain	£9 9s 0d
1859	May 1st "Charles Smout had Money at Different times" His account for the year's wage was:-	
	May 1	10s 0d
	May 14	£2 0s 0d
	Paid the shoemaker	16s 0d
	Shrewsbury Show	5s 0d
	Paid for a watch	£1 10s 0d
	Paid for a broadhook	2s 6d
	Stretton Michelmas Fair	16s 6d
	" " "	2s 6d
	" " "	1s 0d
	" " "	3s 0d
	At Crismas	£1 0s 0d
	At "	2s 0d
	Paid the shoemaker	14s 6d
	" " "	2s 0d
	" " "	5s 0d
	" " "	10s 0d
	Settled with Charles Smout	£9 0s 0d

As can be seen, his annual wage was increased, slightly, each year. His major expenses seem to have been shoe repairs and he must have had quite a time at the Stretton Fair!

1857	May 14 I Hired John Laley for one year	£2 10s 0d
1858	May 14 Hired Robert Rogers for one year	£3 0s 0d

Men from the village were also employed by John Croxton, in addition to those at the Hiring Fair. For example:-

1830	January 1st Thomas Hammond began to work with me at			
	2s 0d a week 40 weeks	£4	0s	0d
	3s 0d a week 52 weeks	£7	16s	0d
	3s 6d a week 12 weeks	£2	5s	6d
		£14	1s	6d
	My Bill against him			
	Settled with Tho Hammond up to Christmas 1832	£13	14s	8d
	due to him		5s	10d

Not a lot after two years' work! However, it records that from January 1st 1832, "he is to have 4s a week".

Earning your living was hard and not a very rewarding task.

In 1852 - Paid for Digen in the Garden		
a man for 4 days	6s	0d
a man for 2 days	3s	0d
The vegetable sown at the time:		
3/2 bushels of Tatters	10s	6d
3 quarts of Beans	1s	0d
Seeds		10d

On a bigger scale is the record of the piece work rate for a drainage system (see illustration).

It was required "to cut the drains 3 feet deep, the pipes laid and the drain filled" for one farthing a yard. A gang of men were employed, each drain being 24 feet apart and, on average, measuring about 200 yards each, 4s 2d for what must have been some very hard work.

Upon the death of a householder it was quite common for 'the effects' to be sold by auction. These occasions were attended by local villagers who bought odd items more as a gesture of friendship than actual need. One sees the same sort of thing today at small farm dispersal sales.

The two following accounts give an idea of prices around 1830.

"Bought by Auction 17 June 1830

Melting tub		5s	3d
A Cask		4s	0d
Market pail		2s	11d
Iron fender		3s	0d
		15s	1d

1830 - 30 Hour Clock	£2	5s	0d
Brass kettle		10s	0d
Brass Pan		10s	0d
Churn		8s	0d
Small casks		6s	0d
Joint stool		3s	0d
2 chairs, 1 arm do		4s	0d
Oak stand		3s	0d
Old stand		1s	0d
Boiler		4s	0d
Mash tub		3s	0d
Pillar & Claw table		5s	0d
Cow & calf	£9	0s	0d
Pair of bellows		1s	0d
	£14	3s	0d

Many families had, in addition to their own family, lodgers to live with them, and the Croxtons were no exception. An account reads:-

"In 1827 Samuel Bowen came to live at my house 20 of July to pay 1 shilling a week." (He later went to live at a cottage near Cwms Farm).

"In 1832 Aug. 31 John Wray came to live in my house at one shilling per week. 5 shillings for the garden a year.
65 weeks he has been there up to last December

paid to me	£2	0s	0d
Due	£1	10s	0d

Drained Winter 1850–51

Bates 119 yards
Beddoes 232 yards
John Price 234 yards
Gittins 235 yards
James Price 233 yards
Corbet 233 yards
Wm Baynham jun 230 yards
Mullard 224 yards
Beddoes 220 yards
John Price 217 yards
Stallard 213 yards
Bates 206 yards
Gittins 200 yards
Corbet 195 yards
Beddoes 190 yards
Mullard 185 yards
Wm Baynham Jr 179 yards
James Price 175 yards
Bates 170 yards
Gittins 127 yards

Beddoes and 178 yards Wm Baynham Junr

Mullard 71½ yards

No on Parish Map 2046 } Long Rough A R P 6·0·30
No on Private Map 74 }

The drains are cut three feet deep and twenty four feet apart. The Pipes were laid and the drains filled by Wm Baynham Junr for one farthing per yard.

1850/51 example of an old drainage system.

In 1841 Richard Poston was paying 13 pence a week and when Robert Lewis came in 1859 the weekly charge was up to 1s 3d, and this rate seems to have remained unchanged for many years as, in 1862, George Grainger was also paying one shilling and three pence a week and 5s 0d a year for the Garden. A Month notice to quit.

In 1898 there is reference to an apprenticeship at Croxton's, the blacksmith:-

> B. Croxton, blacksmith, will agree to take Philip Wallader as apprentice to the above trade, to lodge, board and clothe him for a term of 4 years dating from June 24 1898 which time he has served a trial. Mr. Croxton receiving £15 premium in consideration thereof."

LOCAL LAWS AND TAXES

Military service, or the 'availability of those willing to engage to serve as a volunteer' was a regular demand on each Parish, and in the form dated 1803 addressed to the Constablewick of Hope Bowdler, it is interesting that among the exceptions to serve were clergymen, doctors and Quakers. The infirm and lame were also excluded. Failure to make this return carried a penalty of ten pounds.

The local Justices of the Peace were, among their many other duties, responsible for the poor and destitute souls in the village. The Justices were usually local squires and large landowners, being selected by the Lord Lieutenant of the County, and as well as being responsible for justice, the upkeep of the roads and workhouses, they also levied the rates.

The Rev. W. Marsh, who was inducted as Vicar of Hope Bowdler in 1806, declared that for about four years after he came to the benefice he received from his predecessor 12s yearly to be distributed in bread to the poor, 6s to be given in money on Saint Thomas's Day (21st December), that upon the death of his predecessor 24 years before he applied to his representatives for the principal and ultimately received from them £18. He added £4 to make up £22. He pays 22s thereof as the interest and distributes 12s yearly in bread and 10s in money on St. Thomas's Day.

Until 1843 the Justices had administered relief to the poor, then the Poor Law Guardians system was set up and the responsibility fell to each village with two men - local farmers or landowners - being made Overseers of the Poor. They, together with Churchwardens and the Rector, were also responsible for setting the rates to cover local requirements, the finances of the Church and payments to the King. This system continued until elected Parish Councils were eventually instituted in 1894.

An entry in the Poor Account of 1760 reads:-

"Pd to Kadwallader when he was sick	
4 weeks 1s per week	4s 0d
Pd the Chife Conble	2s 8½
Pd Mary - sister	13s 0d
for surching the ?	1s 0d
Pd to John Kadwallader 18 weeks	18s 0d
for making the coffin	4s 0d
the Clarke fees	3s 0d
Pd the Chife Conble	2s 8½
the poor on St Thomsday	1s 0d

A

Subdivifion of *Munslow* in the County of Salop. } To ... of the *Constablewick* of *Hope Bowdler* in the said Subdivision.

TAKE NOTICE, That you are hereby required, within two Days from the Date hereof, to prepare or produce a Lift in Writing, to the beft of your Belief, of the chriftian and furname of each and every man refident in your dwelling-houfe between the ages of *seventeen* and *fifty five*, diftinguifhing in fuch lift the feveral particulars mentioned in the columns thereof; and in the laft column of remarks fpecify whether the perfon oppofite to whofe name the remark fhall be made is "willing to engage to ferve as a volunteer under this Act, *or* is infirm, or lame, *or* a clergyman, or licenfed teacher in holy orders, Quaker, or medical man, *or* is actually ferving as an officer in the Army, Navy, Marines, Militia, Fencibles, *or* Volunteers, or additional Military Forces, *or* a conftable, or other peace office;" and you are to fign fuch lift with your own name, and to deliver or caufe the fame to be delivered to me. Dated the *eighth* Day of *August*, 1803.

Names.	Defcription.	Age.	Married or Single.	Number of Children under 10 Years.	REMARKS.
A. B.	Houfekeeper		Single		Enrols himfelf in the parifh of L. in the county of M.
C. D.	Servant		Single	None	— —
E. F.	Lodger		Married.	None	— —
G. H.	Inmate		Single	None	Infirm and lame
I. K.	Houfekeeper		Married	1	Voluntary Service

N. B. If any houfe is divided in diftinct ftores or apartments occupied diftinctly, each diftinct occupier is to make this return.—Neglect of compliance with this notice will fubject the party to the penalty of ten pounds.

Take Notice, That the *25th* Day of Auguft, 1803, at the hour of ten the forenoon, is appointed for hearing appeals within this fubdivifion, by perfons claiming to be exempt from ferving.

Constable.

Names.	Defcription.	Age	Married Single.	Number of Children under 10 Years.	REMARKS.

1803 Official form in respect of "availability" for service as a volunteer.

In 1834 there was a Complaint by Richard Wilding and John Rogers (Ragdon and Chelmick farmers), Overseers of the Poor against George Watkin Marsh (Vicar of Hope Bowdler): "Whereas G W Marsh of the Parish of Hope Bowdler being an occupier of Tithes within the said Parish and duly rated in the said Rate the sum of Twenty six pounds and five shillings the said Richard Wilding one of the said Overseers did demand the sum of eighteen pounds and fifteen shillings ... which G W Marsh did neglect and refuse to pay. To appear before the Justices of the Peace at Dorrington on 7th November 1834 at 11.00 a.m."

This was a case where the 'powerful' vicar and his parishioners were at odds. Rev. Marsh seems to have had a somewhat 'troublesome' time during his rectorship, being involved with the High Court in London following the death of W. C. Hart and the sale of the Bowdler Estate and, at a later date, when the Tithe funds were sequestrated by Hereford. A letter from the Clerk dated June 24th 1846 on this matter was very clear and to the point!

> "Sir, it is right that I should inform you that as Mr. Marsh's Rectory is under Sequestration you must not pay him your rent charge in lieu of Tythe.
> I shall attend personally or send to receive the Tythes in due course. Please tell this to any other Parishioners whom you may see.
> I am Sir, Your obedient Servant, Tho. Evans (Sequestrator, Hereford Diocese)"

An example of an account which involved tithe cash payments in 1829 with John Bluck, who farmed the Church lands:

25 April	to John for a pig	0 10 0
16 May	Mrs. Cruxton 2¾ of wool at 1/6	0 4 1
	Loan left unpaid	0 3 0
	Church loan	0 1 9
30 May	12½lb of Pork at 6d	0 6 3
	Mrs. Lewis 1/- for Churching	0 1 0
	Rent of the Church Yard due Lady Day last	0 15 0
	for 2 years Tithe of Broad Beach at 8/- a year	0 16 0
		£2 17 1½

Settled 14 July 'Ann Shaw Bluck'

The provision of names of suitable people to serve on Juries in the County Court fell upon the petty Constable of any given township. The following return is to the County of Salop.

> "The Twentieth Day of Sept. 1742 then John Croxton petty Constable of the township of Hope Bowdler in the said County came before me and made oath before me one of His Majesties Justices of the Peace for the said County that there was no Freeholder nor Leaseholder within this Constablewick Qualifide to serf on Juries. Sworn by me. 'John Croxton'."

An example of medical costs is given below in a Bill from Dr. Richard Wilding (of Church Stretton) for attending the Parish Poor in 1835. The charges appear relatively high but, for some reason, involved travelling to Onibury on a number of occasions.

April 10	Journey to Onibury) Passing catheter &c)	Harrington	10 0
April 11	Journey, passing catheter &c		10 0
April 12	,, ,, ,, ,,		10 0
April 13	,, ,, ,, ,,		10 0
April 14	,, ,, ,, ,,		10 0
			£2 10 0
	Attendance, medicine &c Paupers from Lady Day to Aug. 6 last		1 10 0
			£4 0 0

This relativley early use of a catheter is interesting, the tube was probably made of metal.

The rates of the Parish were assessed on all people who occupied land. The largest contributors were, naturally, the farmers. The assessment for around 1750 on the Parish of Hope Bowdler and the apportionment of the Poor, Church and King is given in the next table. The window tax was also in force, but there appear to be some inconsistencies as some of the calculations of the split of the taxes do not add up exactly!

It is not possible to be certain who the occupants of the farms at Chelmick and Ragdon were at that time, but Mr. Sankey and Mr. Knott were probably at the Chelmick farms, and Mr. Corfield and Mr. Griffiths at Ragdon. Ed Thomas was probably at Upper House Farm, and it is possible that Rev. Adney was living in The Hall and running Lower Farm as the family were no longer living at Ragdon. However, he was not directly connected with Hope Bowdler Church, but his family were Patrons of the Church at this time.

An asesment on the parish of Hope Bowdler circa 1750 4 shiling in ye pound

Poor	*Church*	*King*		*£ s d*	*Windows* *£ s d*
27	0	27	Rev. M. Adney	1 7 0	1 0
31	34	34	Ed Thomas	1 14 0	1 0
11	13	13	Oxc Speck (Speak?)	13 0	1 0
12	13	13	Benjamin Croxton	13 0	1 0
16	16	15	Samuel Croxton	15 0	4 0
12	13	13	Jn Croxton	13 0	1 0
2	2	2	Jn Croxton	2 0	0 0
10	8	8	William Lester	8 0	1 0
8	8	8	Samuel Reagan	8 0	1 0
6	5	6	William Preen	6 0	1 0
0	0	1	Edward Jordan	1 0	0 0

			Chelmick - Ragdon		
25	25	25	Jeremiah Sankey	1 9 0	4 3
26	26	26	Edward Knott	1 6 0	1 0
12	12	11	Thomas Corfield	11 0	1 0
18	18	17	Richard Corfield	17 0	1 0
34	34	39	Richard Griffies	1 19 0	6 7½
5	6	6	Richard Oxenbole	6 0	0 0
2	2	3	Richard Sankey	0 0	0 0

Following the Tithe apportionment register and rateable value, the combined taxes have been dropped and a specified Church Rate levied. In 1838 this was set at 5d in the £1, reduced in 1842 to:

"To Church rate at 3d in the Pound for the year 1842"

Hope Bowdler	*Rateable value*	*Rate*
William Adams	£94 0 0	£1 3 4
John Bluck	53 10 0	13 4
John Croxton	5 0 0	1 3
John Collins	13 10 0	3 4½
Robert Everal	2 5 0	6½
John Broome	2 0 0	6
late William Gorge	10 0 0	2 6
Rowland Galliers	2 10 0	6½
John Griffiths	1 0 0	3
Thomas Jones	12 0 0	3 0
Thomas Oakley	88 10 0	1 2 1½
Thomas Mawn	1 0 0	3
Mathew Hall	1 0 0	3
Samuel Bowen	1 0 0	3
John Sankey	1 10 0	4½
William Williams	1 10 0	4½
James Sheffield	1 0 0	3
Samuel Williams	1 0 0	3
John Wilding	15 0	2
	£293 0 0	£3 12 11
Chelmick & Ragdon		
John Rogers	55 0 0	13 9
Marther Haynes	133 10 0	1 13 4
Thos Wilding	71 10 0	17 8
William Wall	13 0 0	3 3
William Harley	2 0 0	6
John Griffiths	2 0 0	6
Thos Humphries	10 0	1
Richard Cadwallader	1 0 0	3
Widow Ritchard	2 10 0	6½
Thos Griffith	3 0 0	9
Edward Mason	2 10 0	6½
	£286 10 0	£3 11 3

The Window Tax was still in force in 1850 and the Duty per annum was:

8 windows	16 6
9 "	£1 1 0
10 "	£1 8 0
11 "	£1 16 3
12 "	£2 4 9

However, by this date, farm houses with a rateable value under £200 a year were exempt from Window Duty.

The Church Rate rose again in 1860 to 4d in the £1.

Another responsibility of the village was to maintain and pay for the roads of the Parish. The rate varied according to the upkeep required each year and was levied on the rateable value, all farmers and householders being charged.

The account for the 1855/6 expenditure was:

"1855 and 1856 Rode account"

Richard Bennett	32 days	1s 10d a day	£2 13 8
John Howles	1½ days	1s 10d a day	2 9
Thomas Sheffield	48 days	1s 10d a day	4 16 0
Joseph Moile	3½ days	1s 10d a day	5 3
Robert Poston	4 days	1s 10d a day	12 0
17 wagon loads of stone			1 8 4
2 cart loads			1 8
3 days with horses			1 16 0
			£11 15 8

The table showing individual charges for Hope Bowdler residents lists no charges for Chelmick and Ragdon, so it is possible that their roads were, at this time, little more than cart tracks, not requiring upkeep at the expense of the Parish.

John Croxton - Surveyor
Rode rate Four pence in the Pound 1856

	Rateable Value	*Rode rate*
1. William Adams	£201 11 6	£3 7 2½
2. John Pinches	112 0 0	1 17 4
3. Rev. Curtis	22 0 0	7 4
4. John Croxton	33 14 0	11 3¼
5. John Croxton	16 9 0	5 6
6. John Lewis	5 0 0	1 8
7. Francis Gorge	22 0 0	7 4
8. John Jones gdn	2 18 0	11½
9. John Jones	5 16 0	1 11
10. John Carter	22 6 0	10 9½
11. Francis Bishop	203 16 6	3 7 11½
12. J. Evans-Hazler	2 16 0	11

	Rateable value	Rode rate
13. W. Williams	3 4 0	1 1
14. George Poston	2 7 6	9½
15. James Carter	1 12 0	4½
16. Robert Rogers	1 9 6	6
17. - Morgan	1 0 0	4
18. Rev. G. J. Curtis	124 8 0	2 1 5½
		£13 4 8¾

In 1861 the rate was reduced to 3d in the £1.

An indication of the 'poor' state of Hope Bowdler vis-a-vis the other villages is illustrated in this document dated 1756:

"Two Sundays before Michelmase which list must contain the names of all persons within your Constablewick being of the age of one and twenty and under seventy years that have in their possession or trust for them the yearly value of ten pounds or freehold or Coppyhold and leasehold 20 pounds above Reprises or what is payable thereout you must likewise give Notice to the Overseers of the Poor of your several parishes or townships to provide the County rate and deliver the same to me at the time and place Aforesaid which county rates are settled as underwritten, viz:

Acton Scott	11 10½d
Felhampton	13 4½
Wistanstow	2 4½
Strefford	3 4½
Alcaston	3 4
Culmington	5 4½
Shipton	11 8
Burley Bagnorton	6 0½
Hope Bowdler	1 4
Chelmick/Ragdon	1 4½
Whittingslow	4 8
	£3 7 9

24 August 1756"

TRADES AND EMPLOYMENT

The village blacksmith played a very important role, as he, along with the wheelwright, catered for nearly everybody's needs. Naturally shoeing horses, repairing farm implements and the like formed the major part of his work, but from the Day book entries his scope of repairing gates, tools, kitchen utensils and ranges etc. illustrated his value.

In Hope Bowdler the Croxton family, through successive generations, were the blacksmiths from the early 1700's until well into the 20th Century. In addition to his smithy work, a Croxton played other roles in the village life. One of them was Clerk to the Parish for 65 years, as well as being road surveyor, constable, church warden and no doubt involved in raising the monies necessary to keep the Church in repair and to build the school.

In addition to his own sons who worked in the business, we have seen that he employed men to work for him as, for example, blacksmith's striker.

As has been said, times were hard in the 18th and 19th Centuries, and some typical charges were:

1775	Cost of a shoe	0 0 4
	4 removes	0 0 4
1793	2 shoes	0 0 10
	4 shoes	0 1 8
	to mending hames	0 0 1
1797	4 piggs rings	0 0 2
1799	Wilding seting 3 Bullock hornes	0 3 0
1803	Mr. Heynes seting 2 Bullock hornes	0 2 0

This 'seting of bullocks horns' was carried out for nearly all the farmers in the Parish in April or May during the period 1799-1804, then never again. It appears that this was a 'fashion' perhaps to do with showing bullocks at a Fair, and wanting to have the horns symmetrical and to a certain shape. The Master Farriers and Blacksmiths Association explains that the operation involved putting two tubes over the horns, connected to a screw thread which allowed for either expansion or contraction of the space between the horns -

A blacksmith's account for J. Griffiths, a mason, who lived at Chelmick Pools for 1803 reads:

February 3	to steeling a stone axe	0 1 6
	to mending 2 wegges	0 0 2
March 15	to a eye to a mattock	0 2 0

april 29 1803 Set 6 Bullocks horns 6=0
May 18 D Mr Stedman seting 6 Bullocks 6=0
Mr Wainwright seting 4 Bullocks 4=0
Thos. Wide seting 5 Bullocks 5=0
Cartright Slunging 5 Bullocks horns 5=0
Mr Heyns seting 2 Bullocks [illegible] 2=0
Cartright [illegible] seting 5 Bullocks 5=0
1804 Wilding [illegible] seting 2 Bullocks 2 0
august 10 Canfield seting 4 Bullocks 4 0
Sepr 22 Barker seting 4 [illegible] 4 0
29 Mr B Bridgman seting 2 Bullocks 2 0
November 26 Mr Canfield seting 2 Bullock 2 0
December 1 Mr Garritt seting 3 Bullock 3 0
3 Bridgman seting Bullocks horns 1=6
1805 april 22 seting 6 Bullocks horns 6 0
May 28 Canfield seting 6 Bullock [illegible] 6 0
[illegible] seting 4 Bullock horns 4 6
July 15 [illegible] seting 7 Bullock horns 7 0

1803 blacksmith's day book entry for "seting of bullocks horns".

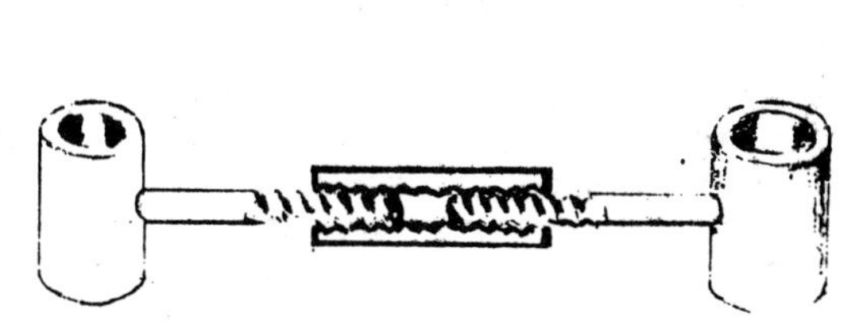

Diagram of apparatus for setting the horns

August 6	to 4 wegges 6¾	0 2 9½
Sept. 11	to steeling and facing a hammer	0 0 8
Sept. 24	you gave me at Stretton	0 4 0

Scythes were, at that time, the only way of cutting corn and there are two references to their making and selling.

1799	July 8	I sould scyth that year 16 at 3s 6d.
1807		I sould scyth that year 27 at 5s 0d.

Business obviously improved over the years.

The annual income of a village blacksmith in the mid-1800s was between £80-90. That was the gross figure, out of which wages had to be paid, materials purchased and his own family had to live. The average yearly bill for farmers with around 130 acres was between £4 and £7. The Haynes family that was farming around 400 acres at one time was the biggest customer at around £16 a year.

Therefore, while it was an important business, it was not really sufficient to produce a decent income so, in addition to farming some rented land, John Croxton also carried out a variety of other work to make a bit more money and to keep the men he employed busy all the year round. Some of the day book entries show the diversity of work undertaken:

1849 July 30	One day horling Fagots for William Harley (of Chelmick Pools) from the Pinches Coppy	0 10 0
1850	3 days threshing	2 5 0
1854	Horling lime & stone to the Turnpike	0 10 0
1855	Ploughing one day	0 10 0
1851 Nov. 10	by the order of Mr. Gorge	
	Half a day horling sand - 3 horses	0 7 6
Nov. 11	Horling 700 bricks	0 7 0
	Gate (Toll)	0 1 6
Nov. 12	Half a day horling sand	
	one load to All Stretton Brig	0 7 6
	450 bricks	0 4 6
	Gate	0 0 8
		£1 8 8
1852	Horling stone	
	one day with 6 horses	1 13 0
	Three load of Pebles	1 0 3
1855	Horling part load of stone and gravel to the Hovel and Bords	0 5 0
	Horling Gate post from Clae Brook	0 3 0
	Plough the Pikes	0 10 0
Dec. 11	Horling Cordwood from Raglet	0 13 0

When John and Elizabeth Croxton first moved to Hope Bowdler in around 1715, they had two sons Shimrah and Bezaleel and four daughters. Bezaleel worked with his father in the blacksmith shop and, upon his death, took over himself. Shimrah, on the other hand, worked as a weaver in the village (as his father had also done as a sideline to his blacksmith work). A few of the account book records have survived which show the variety of his work and the prices.

1772	8 yd of liney at 4	2s 8d	(? lincey)
	9 yd of liney at 2	1s 6d	
	12 yd of liney at 3	3s 0d	
	9 El of horndon at 2	1s 6d	(? hodden, coarse cloth, undyed)
	11 Els of flaxen at 4	6s 4d	
1775	7 yd of Carsey at 4	2s 4d	(? corsey)
1776	12 yd of flanel 1½	1s 6d	
	1 blanket	1s 6d	
	20 yd of Curtain at 4	8s 8d	
	11 Els of Hemton	3s 4d	(a tough fibre)
1777	7 yds of huggabagg at 6	3s 6d	(strong rough linen for toweling)
	4 yd of Chees cloth	1s 0d	
	21 yd of tickin	7s 0d	
1778	June 30 Mr. Morris of Ragdon		
	30 El of hord	5s 2d	(an 'El' was 45")

The weaving shop was not carried on in Hope Bowdler after 1800. Shimrah, who had three daughters, moved to Church Stretton, where he continued weaving and eventually died in 1836 aged 86.

Living alongside the blacksmith's shop throughout the 1800's was a wheelwright business. First, Richard Gallears then, from 1851, John Jones who - with his sons - continued until his death in 1884. There is an amusing story told of John Jones who built a wagon without using any nails, screws or bolts, depending on wooden wedges or pegs. It was, in its way, unique. However, to his chagrin (and the amusement of others) after a very long hot summer, the wooden pegs all came loose and the wagon collapsed.

There must have been plenty of work in the wheelwright and carpentry trade as, in the mid 1850's, James Hammond (who married Mary Croxton) came to live where the Haven is today and also set up business as wheelwright. He had an apprentice carpenter working for him in 1871, and when he died in 1877 his son, Jesse, took over and ran the business and his wife was a laundress. She lived to 82.

The women played an important and hard working role in the family and village life. In the early census returns there are many instances of the occupation of women being given as 'agricultural labourer', particularly among the older ones. They were of course very much involved at haymaking and harvest times.

For the men farming was the biggest employer of labour, but close behind it in numbers came domestic service. There was little employment available to young girls and they went, almost automatically, into service. In country areas, with large houses few and far between, opportunities for local engagement were scarce, and girls had to travel, mainly to London, to find work. Embarking on such journeys to work in large households must have filled many a young girl's heart with terror. The coming of the railway in the mid-1800's made it more practical and less of a hazardous undertaking.

From letters written in the 1860's one gets some idea of what life must have been like for young girls a long way from home. Their family and religion were very important to them, as this extract shows:

> "I now take my pen to write these few lines unto you hopeing you are quite well as this leaves me at present thank God for it Dear Father. I have sent you a small Chrismas present if you will except it Dear Mary said that you wanted some flanall shirts so I thought that ten shillings would buy you som and I wish you a merry Chrismas when it comes if you live to see it Dear Father... I must conclude in hopes you will write as soon as you can and say if you get the ten all saf and right and will you please to write yourself as I should so like a letter from you your own writing. Good by and God Bless you all."
>
> (Nov. 25 1862)

Being away and only able to get home very occasionally made them, naturally, very homesick.

> "I dare say I shall come home in May all been well. Mary Ann say it is no use coming when all the fun is over but I dont know for sure yet it is only what we have been talking about our selfs sometimes I think I never can wait till then I often dream of home till it makes me feel quite vexed when I wake to think I am so far from home."
>
> (Cavendish Square, London, 1864)

The work was often hard, but the life below stairs was not all drudgery, and the number of staff employed must have been considerable:

> "I fear all of you will think it very unkind for me not writing to you before but I really have not had time till to night and now I am very much tired after a hard day work and then a jolly Danse to finish up with ... I know I have no time for anything so tell Mary she must not expect me to write her nor none of the others for while little time I have after scrubing pans they come and fetch us out of the kitchen into the Hall for a Dance."
>
> (1866)

Life also had its problems and nervousness about the future is well summed up in this extract:

> "I thought I would write and tell you I am leaving here for I cannot stay with Mrs. Bland any longer for she is dreadful there is 6 leaving 3 of us through that old beast ... is a very bad time of year for a Place now in

London so I dont know how I shall get on as I am not overstocked with money not for London I hope I shall soon get a place some where but I feel very nervous about it as I don't like moving."

(Goldings, Pitchford, c.1866)

And the chance to come home was something to write home about:

"In haste I write to tell you all I am coming home on Saturday next to remain in Shropshire till the following Wensday all been well the train comes right to Church Stretton so I think I cant spen 10 shillings better for I dont care for goin any were up here (in London) as I dont know anyone here and I want a little change ... I am coming by the Great Western line I like that much better than the other the time will be very short but I would rather come for that short time than stop here twice as long though there is so much to see every day."

(Cavendish Square, 1865)

While they certainly learnt something of housekeeping practice, they also seem to have had an eye for making a little money on the side:

"I think I shall like it although it is very hard but plenty to lern if I have luck to stop, The kills most all there own meat and carry all a sheep into the kitchen for the cook to cut up ½ a beef at time besides other things I never was so surprised in all my life since I have been here I had no idea that there was all the meat and things so much differin than I have I think that a good deal I have the bones and Hare and rabbit skins for my prequisites I made 14 since Thursday I hope I can take the work I wish some of you could peep and see me sometime you would think me mad."

It was not only the daughters who went away to find work, there were many cases where sons could not find employment either in the family business or locally and set out to find their fortune elsewhere. A letter dated 1870 has some poignant comments on the thoughts of one such young man:

"I was thinking about you and all the new years day, thinking what jolly times we where used to have years gone by I thought very much about home (dear old home) that day more than ever I did I could not get it out of my head do or think about whatever I would and I was very sorry to leave home at first but I know that there was not there for me so I thought when I was young that was the best time to try so I think I have acted the right road though I thought it very hard at first no one knew my feelings beside myself when Zeal parted with me at Wenlock four years next July, time soon flys away it only seems as yesterday I never shall forget the day, though I think every one ought to go out from home when young to see what the world is although it tis very hard to part from friends that anyone has been with all their days I should not have cared so much if I could have overcome one thing and that I never shall but I very much trust to providence and He will provide for me and every ones else that puts their whole trust in Him. In hope that you gone to Church regular and never mind a bit of cold (but go) ... Believe me to be your affectionate son (be sure to go to church)."

FARMING

Farming in the area had been the only way of life and occupation for most of the population for centuries. It has never been a prosperous region and, because of this, life or living had been in a very depressed state for years. The murrain or pestilence among the sheep had caused near ruin in the 18th and 19th centuries.

In Mediaeval times the area was heavily wooded and the Domesday Book specifically refers to 'two leagues of wood' among the taxable assets of the village.

In December 1222 an account is given that "a great storm had devastated England and uprooted so many trees that the normal customs of dealing with trees were suspended. The Long Forest was oak and hazel. Records of venison offences show that red deer predominated in the forests of Shropshire."

In the local register dated 22 July 1804 appears:

"Awful tremendous storm of thunder and lightning. Hail and rain. Hail fell in the neighbourhood from 1 to 4 inches in length resembling broken ragged ice. The wheat cut off by the head, windows destroyed everywhere the hail could reach. In short it was an *awful visitation.* May it ever be remembered in this neighbourhood."

Towards the end of the 18th century a big change in agriculture occurred with the scale and pace of 'the enclosures' which swept village communities into the beginning of the world of commercial farming, when the scattered strips and common pasture were brought into a series of compact and consolidated holdings. The farmer who could establish title to a series of arable strips scattered among the open fields, and who consequently exercised rights in the common grazings, could expect to receive in the enclosure award a compact block of land equivalent to his scattered strips and an allotment which was supposed to equal his common pasture rights.

Shropshire passed into enclosure silently and much earlier than many other counties.

The Enclosure Act adversely affected many people lower down the farming scale. The first to go were those who lacked a permanent title to the strips which they rented, landlords were in no way obliged to offer them new holdings within compacted or enclosed fields. Cottagers who rented cottages which by ancient custom carried rights to the common grazings usually went uncompensated when the commons were enclosed. He was now unable to support the odd beasts and was thus deprived of milk, meat and muck for his garden and arable crops. His rights to timber were also often lost. He now needed cash for all the goods he had to buy, instead of provide for himself, and was left with only one thing to sell - his labour.

That was how the general pattern of agriculture stood in the early 1800's. In a report on farms in Hope Bowdler around this time, one or two were described as "in pretty good" or "tolerable" repair, but the majority were in a "poor state". The land was not being farmed well, often being described as in an "indifferent state of culture".

One of the reasons for this poor state of the land was the need to carry out draining in both the pasture and arable fields. The report goes on to say that the Landlord "should be liberal" in doing this and "the Tenant to carry the stones". Many fields today still have these original stone drains, though most are now silted up and defunct, and these have been superceded, first by tile drains and later the perforated plastic continuous piping. The task of digging (to 3′ deep) and filling with stone go give good drainage was a laborious, backbreaking and time consuming job and, as has been mentioned earlier, the piecework rate was at one time only ¼d a yard.

In some cases full draining was not considered necessary and "a few gutters cut in the land would improve it very much" but the tenant in one case "had not sense enough to perceive that it would benefit him."

An example of ingenuity and effort to improve crops was carried out in Chelmick Valley. Along the western side, about halfway up the slope, can still be seen a ridge or pathway running from the Pools to the Birtley end. This was, in fact, a ditch dug out by hand along which water was diverted in Springtime to irrigate the meadows, so that a hay crop could be taken off the lower fields.

The growing of turnips and clover were a very important part of the crop rotation practised then. Leaving fields fallow was also part of the rotation, but there were many cases where this was done simply because that farmer could not afford to cultivate every field. Reference is made to one piece of land in a foul state, saying "they have grown 4, 5, 6 and 7 crops in succession, enough to ruin any land whatsoever."

A suggestion to one farmer read "By pursuing a more regular course of Turnip husbandry, always sowing a sufficient quantity of mixed clover seed with the grain crop that follows the turnips, letting it remain in pasture two years before it is again broken up."

By the time of the Tithe Award of 1843 there has been a large scale conversion from pasture to arable farming. In fact, a glance at the Tithe map (see next page) shows that there was more arable in the Parish at that time than there is today. The actual sizes of the seven farms is little different from today, but there were several cottages with a few acres each - slightly at odds with the general situation referred to earlier. The cottagers worked as agricultural workers and some of the references to their stock, with no mention of any charges, shows some goodwill by the different farmers.

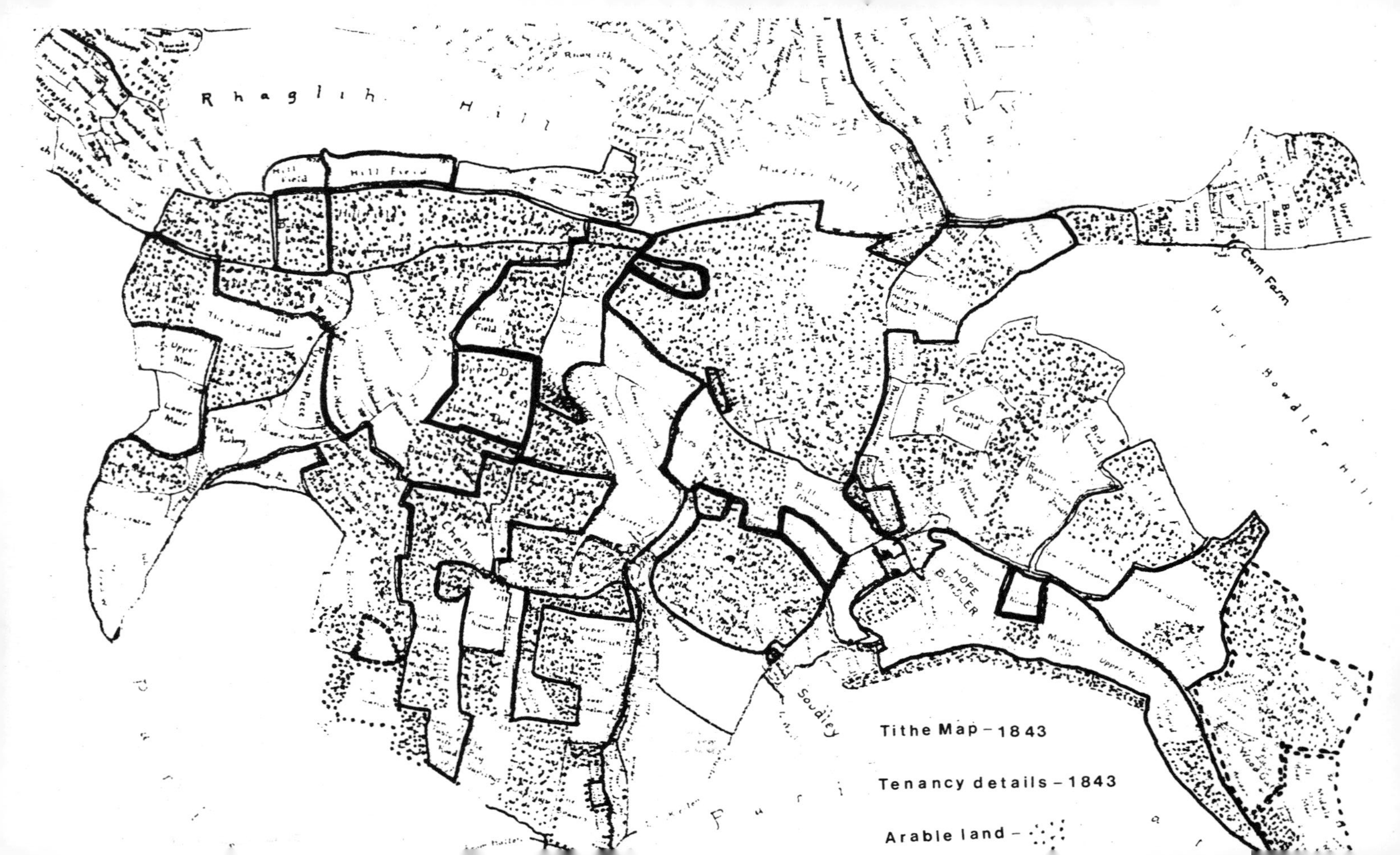

Rhaglih Hill
Hazler Hill
Hope Bowdler Hill
Cwm Farm
Hill Field
Barley Butts
Garden Field
Cross Field
Upper Dol
Lower Dol
Upper Moor
Lower Moor
The Ford Head
Ryegrass Piece
The Pike Furlong
Chelmick
HOPE BOWLER
Cole Ground
Coldshot Field
Bird Lacel
House Meadow
Banky Meadow
Bull Meadow
Soudley
Tithe Map – 1843
Tenancy details – 1843
Arable land –

1831	The cow had Mr Adams bull 13 of July	
	My cow took Mises Haynes bull August 7	
	Mare took the horse 24 of July	
1855 June 9	the yurling heifer took Mr Adams bull	
,, 28	the Ragdon cow took Mr Brits bull	
1867 July 5	The gilt took Mr Faulkner's boar	
1857 June 24	Shipton cow took Mr Wildings bull	
,, 27	Chelmick cow took Mr Wildings bull	
Aug. 11	,, ,, ,, ,, ,, ,,	second time

Below are some examples of prices realised at this time:

1824 July 3	Sold 7 stone of wooll for	£6 10 0
	Sold 5 hens at 13d a peace	5 5
	3 wether sheep	6 5 0
	Lames wooll	1 0 0
	2 sheep we ad killed	1 0 0
		£15 0 5
1825 July 3	Sold 8 stone of wooll	£8 10 0
	10pd of lames wooll	12 6
	1pd of Britchen wooll	6 8
	6 wether sheep at 23s a peace	
	3 hewes at 16s a peace and	
	one Tup at £1	10 6 0
		£19 15 2
1829	Sold a colt £2 10 0	
	sold a mare 1 5 0	
1830	sold 2 pigs 15 0	
1831 Nov 16	Bought 2 trees of Mr Hart at one pound	
1853 Febury	Shrewsbury Fair	
	Sold a fat pig	£5 5 0
Mar 7	sold a fat cow	14 0 0
,, 14	Sold 2 cows and calves	
	one at	12 10 0
	and other at	10 5 0
July 3	sold 2 Bulocks for	14 5 0
	sold the flece wooll	
	at 15d a lb 2c95lb	18 18 0
	sold a colt	15 0 0
		£101 3 0
1854	sold the Duke Horse	£29 0 0

In most parts of England, village population reached its peak around 1860, and the years that followed saw the beginning of an exodus from the village toward the town. This was due partly to the pull of higher wages and better housing offered in the factory and the town, and partly to the fall in farming employment. In 1861 the English countryside provided work for almost two million farmers and labourers, but by 1901 this was halved. The fall in jobs was partly caused by the seasonal nature of farm work, rather than employ a large labour force who would often be idle during the winter months, farmers discovered the profits to be made by reducing the permanent workforce to the minimum. During the busy weeks of summer extra hands were recruited from Irish harvest gangs who came over for haymaking and harvest and, of course, the women of the village could be called on to help. Mechanisation began to erode the village workforce still further, by 1870 reaping machines and later the mechanical reaper-binder began to replace the swishing scythe, and it also did away with the tying of sheaves which had employed women and children. Also, these machines more or less put an end to the gleaning of the harvest field which had enriched the family grain store.

An interesting record of some of the work of Richard Jones (of Chelmick Pools) and his two sons who, as well as running a smallholding themselves, worked on a day/jobbing basis for many of the farmers in the area.

They were certainly versatile in the work they took on as the following extracts from their Day Books show, as well as giving a picture of the wages and charges of the day.

1876 Oct. 2nd	Beating 1 day for Mr Benson	2s 6d
1879 May	Hauling building stone for Mr Wilding Ragdon	1s 0d a load
1879 July	Feeding machine (threshing) at Mr Wilding 1 day	2s 0d
1879 July 24	Mr George, Wood Gate Farm shearing 1 day (in 1873 it had been 2s 6d a day)	3s 0d
1880 June 21	Washing sheep Mr Wilding 1 day	3s 0d
” 22	Shearing 16 sheep Rev Benson	4s 4d
1880	Thatching 1 day	3s 0d
1881 Dec 12	Mr Heynes Ragdon, thatching Wain House (cart shed) 4½ days	12s 9d
1882 May 30	Thatching J Carter's cottage Soudley (later burnt down)	10s 0d
1882 May 31	Chelmick Manor, Altering ironwork & hanging gate	2s 6d

At this time mechanical reapers or binders were a rarity and at hay making and harvest time they were engaged for mowing with scythes.

1880 Aug 2	Mowing 10 acres grass	£3	0	0
” 14	Cutting grass Mr Wilding 2 days		5	0
1881 Aug 15	Mr Rogers Chelmick. Making up hay, stacking, 3½ days		8	0

1881 Aug 26	Men cutting barley	
	R Jones ⅓ day	1 10
	P Jones ½ day	1 0
	R Jones 3¼ days	8 1½
	P Jones 2¼ days	4 6
	(note: Richard charged 2s 6d a day and his 18 year old son Philemon 2s 0d)	

The Jones had, at one time, also been woodsmen and they did a lot of work for the Hope Bowdler and Lutwyche Estates. There are many entries for felling and planting trees on Helmeth and Bowdler Hills, making stakes, cutting cordwood and fagots. There are many references to ash, larch and oak and the large quantities involved showed how heavily wooded this area still was in those days. The timber value was mentioned in the Domesday Book. There was, later, some heavy felling of trees in the Great War.

1886 May 3	R B Benson	
	Longville timber, bark peeling, ranking and loading 53 tons 16cwt 32pd	£85 19 3
	The men were paid 2s 10d a day.	
1886 July 2	Felling and rounding 4,560ft Oak at 10/- per hd (100)	£22 16 0
1887 Jan 10	Elmeth Coppice	
	cutting 1,120 stakes at 1/6 a hd	16 9
	1hd + 94 faggots at 7/- a hd	12 6
Feb 11	100½ cords of wood at 3/-	£16 4 9
1888 Dec.	Falling 600 larch at Hope Bowdler	£11 0 0

Some of the hardest work must have been in the saw pits. There were two in Hope Bowdler, where the pay was 3/6 a day, higher than for any other work at the time.

An example of the work records for saw pit work reads:

"Sawing by Measure" Mar 20 1868

Cuts	long	bredth	feet
5	6½'	14"	37'11"
		1 crosscut	10'
12	6½'	9"	59'
3	7½'	11"	20'6"
		1 crosscut	10'
10	7½'	9"	55'10"
3	6½'	11"	17'9"
		1 crosscut	5'
9	6½'	9"	43'6"
6	16½'	12"	99'6"

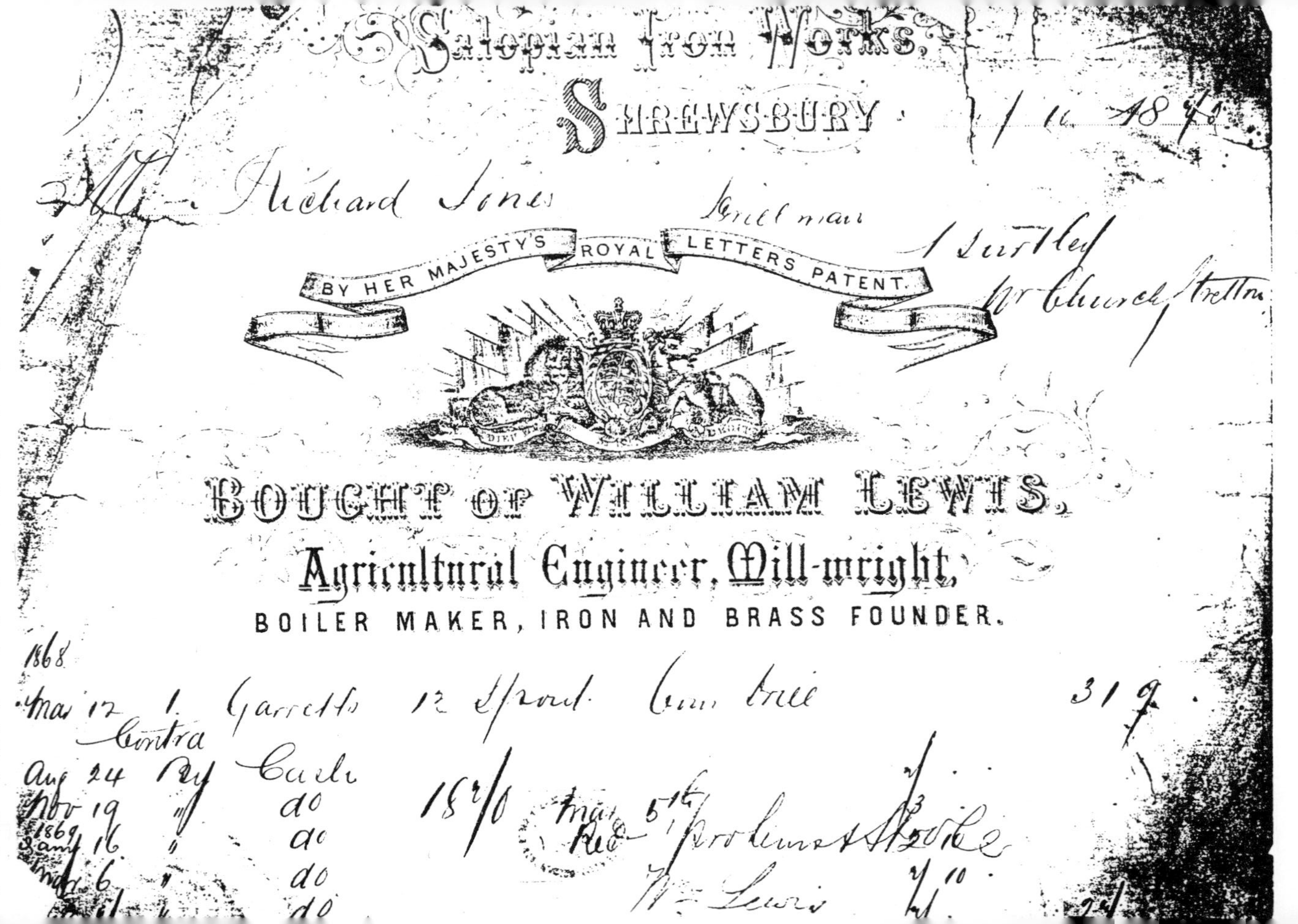

Salopian Iron Works,
Shrewsbury.

Mr Richard Jones

BY HER MAJESTY'S ROYAL LETTERS PATENT.

Bought of William Lewis,
Agricultural Engineer, Mill-wright,
BOILER MAKER, IRON AND BRASS FOUNDER.

Facsimile of the invoice for the first mechanical seed drill for Richard Jones.

The previous examples give some idea of the diversity of the work carried out, there was one aspect of farming at that time which Richard Jones was able to claim a very definite first in the area, and that was mechanical drilling.

Up to that time the sowing of crops had been carried out by broadcasting or the hand operated seed fiddle. Both time consuming and not particularly efficient in the actual usage of seed.

What Richard Jones did was to buy one of the very first mechanical drills from William Lewis of the Salopian Iron Works in Shrewsbury on March 12th 1868 and was invoiced as "Richard Jones, Drillman, 1 Garrett 13 spout Corn Drill £31 9 0"

With this drill he set out to carry out contract drilling, not only for the smallholders but also for most of the large farmers in and around the Parish. His charge was one shilling an acre and this price remained unchanged for the next twenty years. The account books show just two exceptions to this charge - when he drilled 3½ acres of wheat for Mr. Wilding the surgeon in Church Stretton and for the work he did over four years when Chelmick Manor was in the hands of the Executors - for these he charged 50% more, 1s 6d an acre.

There was a wide variety of crops being grown - oats, barley, wheat, rye, peas, turnips and vetches. From the records it is obvious that they must have had some bad weather years. For example in 1868 3 acres of barley was being put in as late as June 1st, and then at the end of that year 8 acres of wheat was drilled for Mr. Heynes of Ragdon on December 18th.

Evidence of the small farm at Dryhill growing crops other than potatoes were the entries for a 2 acre field being drilled with oats and barley in different years.

The more general use of seed drills, the arrival of steam engines with their multi-furrow tip up one-way ploughs and cultivators, the threshing machines doing in a day what used to occupy the winter days of the workers flailing the corn on the threshing floor. Finally, when the tractor arrived in the 1920's, began the last chapter of farming as it had been known up to then, vanquishing both the horse and the steam engine in the next few decades.

This change is dramatically illustrated as far as the Hope Bowdler Parish is concerned. In 1880 there were 28 houses with a total of 57 men and women regularly working on farms. Today, just over 100 years later, there are 63 houses and just 12 people working in farming.

FIELD-NAMES

The composite map of Hope Bowdler Parish, (see overleaf) shows all the individual fields by their tithe award number and name, these in turn can be compared with the Tithe apportionment details of 1843 contained in Appendix 1.

In preparing this chapter on some of the field-names in the Parish, I have referred extensively to "Shropshire Field-names" by H D G Foxall and, as it states in the introduction, many of the explanations offered are purely conjectural.

The old fields were all given names that had a meaning to those living on or working the land, and those listed here probably originate around 1750-1800, many may be even older.

Study of these names give a better understanding of the local history, the people, the varieties of crops grown, the landscape and where old buildings once stood. It would be tedious to refer to every field and there are some for which a meaning cannot be traced, but the following are interesting and in some cases are associated with references elsewhere in the text.

Several words occur frequently and have a general meaning.

LEASOW means pasture land and comes from the OE (old English) LAESWE - in Shropshire it is pronounced LEZZOW.

CROFT and CLOSE - the name generally given to small fields surrounding or adjoining small crofts and cottages. However, on some Shropshire tithe maps, as in Hope Bowdler, they appear as quite large, isolated fields.

FURLONG - the basic unit of cultivation was the long narrow strip and these were arranged in units called furlongs from the OE FURLANG. A furlong was a group of strips - all the same length - a furlong or furrow long. This was the length of furrow that could be ploughed by a team of oxen without stopping to take rest. Length was important to give a good run for the plough and because of the difficulty of turning the ponderous plough and its unwieldy team at the end of the strips. The length of the furlong varied, but eventually it was standardised as a unit of length at 40 poles or 220 yards. The width of the individual strip was fixed at 4 poles or 22 yards. This amounted to one acre, and was considered to be a day's ploughing.

The fact that much of the area was, at one time, covered by forest or woodland and is of a hilly nature is clearly illustrated by some of the names.

BIRD LAUREL (tithe number 36) - after the tree 'Bird Cherry', Prunus Padus.

STOW BATCH (38) - although this is written on the tithe map as 'Stow', this could be an error as its earlier name is recorded as 'How', and this could have been a batch or wood of Alder trees as this tree has many names in Shropshire as well as Howler are Ollers and Wallers in common use.

STOCKING (209/210) - means land covered with stocks or tree stumps.

COPY PIECE (257) - coppiced woodland after the felling of mature trees.

YELLS (69,70/3/4/8) from the OE HELDE - 'a slope'.

HANGING MEADOW (30) - a hillside from the OE HANGENDE.

FERNEY LEY (32) - this probably should read 'Ferry', derived from the OE FIERGEN - a wooded hill or OE FIEREL - a place growing with oaks. This view is reinforced by the fact that many of the oldest field-names referring to cleared forest land, brought into cultivation, ended in 'ley'.

Other examples of the open, barren nature of the landscape are -

GORSTY FIELD (40) - a gorse bank.

BROOMY FIELD (44/5) - in an exposed position.

THE MOORS (147/8,157) - low lying marshy land, rather than expanses of gorse and heather. This is a Shropshire meaning.

BROTCHES (258,260/1/2) - land newly broken and brought into cultivation, usually taken from heathland.

The type of fodder crops grown is reflected in fields like CHICKERY (132), UPPER FEG (224) - a type of grass, VETCH (246), TURNIP LEASOW (197), CABBAGE FIELD (58/9) and RYE GRASS PIECE (282).

Many of the other names cannot be classified into any particular groups, but each has a local meaning.

COCKSHUTT FIELD (88d) - a hillside spring or rivulet from which water was carried by a spout or trough. LIGHT SPOUT (88g) is by the road, just above the village and may have a similar meaning.

BOUNTAIL (88f) - this was possibly a boundary field from an earlier division of the land. In the tax assessment of 1843 it was written as 'Brantail' which could have been after the bird-name of a Redstart.

COTE GROUND (31/90) - this could be from the OE COT - a cottage, hut or shed for animals. As no house is recorded here, an animal shelter is possible, but the 18th Century name was 'Goat Ground' which seems more likely.

Rhaglith Wood
Rhaglith Hill
Hill Field
Ox Pasture
The Shop Leasow
Dry Hill
Inclosure
Hazler Field
Cainall
Hazler Close
Broomy Leasow
Lower Cainall
The Stocking
Lower Stocking
Moors
The Moors
Big Cold Hill
Quarry Leasow
Further Dales
Near Dales
Butchers Leasow
Piece above Road
Near Marrols
Near Ditch Field
The Old Yard
Near Old Field
Colliers Yard
Ragdon
Barn Yard
Cow Pasture
Far Cross Field
Near Cross Field
Sideland Cold Hill
Spring Piece
Spring Coppy
Little Cold Hill
Upper Dol
Lower Dol
Meadow
The Yard Head
Ryegrass Piece
Garden Meadow
Stackyard Meadow
The Hearne
Upper Feg Field
Lower Feg Field
Sheep Pasture
Upper Moor
The Little Moors
Barn Yard
Lower Moor
The Pine Furlong
Sideland Meadow
Backside Leasow
Ditch Cop
Further Ditch
Ditch Cop
Bradley Furlong
The Sleeve
Backside
Vetch Stubble
The Little Backside
Knowle Stock
Backside Field
Little Biglow Field
Biglow
Quarry
Rag Butch
Brand Leasow Yard
Further Broad Leasow
Further Yard
Chelmick
Pool or Moor Leasow
Briery Leasow
Tinkers Meadow
Upper Hatch
Pike Meadow
Broad Meadow
Lower Leasow
Barn Yard
Upper Mill Leasow
Little Cote Leasow
Upper Chelmick
The Big Cote Leasow
Lower Chelmick
Hatch Meadow
For Brotches
The Brotches
Lower Brotches Coppice
The Pikes
Hill Headlands
Goodings Meadow
The Coppy Piece
The Old Lands
Cow Pasture with Road
The Pikes
The Big Saplings
The Upper Little Saplings
The Lower Saplings
The Spawns
From Halton
Plantation
Coppice
Upper Plecks
Snatch Field
Pleck
Hazler Land
Wood
Lower Plecks
Hazler Hill
Coles Wood
Line
Broomy Field
Poges Ground
Hangings Piece
Marsh
Heley Leasow
Brickkiln Leasow
Garretts Pool
Pasture

Hope Bowdler Hill
Cwm Farm
HOPE BOWDLER
Soudley
To Wall
To Wall
Toll Gate
Whistlement
Whistlement
Hopes Corner
Turnpike Field
Near Turnpike Field
Middle Field
Gorden Field
Barn Yard
Barley Butts
Upper Knowles
Middle Knowles
Lower Knowles
The Meadow
Upper Hanging Meadow
Hanging Meadow
Cote Ground
Cote Ground
Lady Field Leasow
Old House Leasow
Ferny Ley
Flat Meadow
Bird Laurel
Gorsty Field
Cockshut Field
Wall Leasow
Robins Rough
Little Ment
Yewtree Field
Banky Meadow
The Patches
Harpers Close
House Meadow
Light Spout
Yewtree Meadow
Tinkers Ground
Big Broomy Field
Little Broomy Field
Great Meadow
Cote Meadow
The Yells
Brick Kiln Field
Near Brick Kiln Field
Quarry Leasow
Upper Part of Shed
Lower Part of Shed
Little Yells
Middle Yells
Upper Yells
The Long Yells
Plantation
Field
Mount Flirt
Upper Mount Flirt
The Rickyard Field
Little Meadow
Evans Meadow
Mead Furlong
Hollow Meadow
Townsend
Large Inclosure
Big Meadow
Wood Gate
Cabbage Field
Small Field
Fox Gill Moor
Middle Gill Moor
Lower Gill Moor
The Meadow

LADY FIELD (33) - 'Lady' can indicate land dedicated to the Virgin Mary for the maintenance of some shrine or chapel.

RACKLESS (88c) - could mean a field without stones, a rarety in the area, but as it was written as 'Rackles' in the tax assessment it could mean a 'rough footpath' from the OE HRAĆA.

TINKERS GROUND (75/302) - are both near roads and is probably where they would have camped on their way across country.

BRICKKILN (68/68a) - indicates sometime brick making.

MILL HILL (140) - together with the reference to 'Mill Pool Meadow' in the sale details of the Thomas Chelmick' property in 1635, suggests that there was probably a mill located there at one time.

DUNSTALL (141) may refer to the site of a farmhouse from the OE TUN-STALL, usually to be found on the borders of ancient wastes, as if they had been outlying farmyards without homesteads.

THE BUTTRESSES (138/143) can refer to shooting or archery butts, but unlikely to be the case here. It more likely refers to fields belonging to more than one person, a butt being a space of ploughed land comprising a certain number of furrows.

DOL (221) - a meadow called, in Welsh Border counties, a 'Dol' or 'Gweirglodd'. The fields at Ragdon are the furthest east recorded.

CHURCHYARD MEADOW (271) as it is remote from the Parish Church it is unlikely to have any religious connection, but it could be because skeletons were once found there.

OLD SHOP LEASOW (216) - an old shed, and not a shop for the sale of goods.

THE GUINEA MEADOW (203) - possibly connected to the money paid for work carried out there at some time.

Many of the names refer to the shape of fields. THE SLEEVE (207) long and narrow; THE HEARNE (268) a field with many corners; SOUDLEY SPAWNS from the OE SPANN - 'a span or hands-breadth' may well refer to narrow strips of land; SLANG (169) a narrow strip and PIKES (254) sharp cornered.

The people who owned or farmed certain fields often gave their names like HARPERS CLOSE (92), ROBINS ROUGH (37), EVANS MEADOW (121), WALKERS CLOSE (111), BUTCHERS LEASOW (293) and so on.

Many of these old names have now been lost as fields have been merged together to make larger units to suit modern farming requirements, and some have disappeared to accommodate the building of new houses.

THE SCHOOL

It was not until 1856 that a school was built in Hope Bowdler. Before this children would have had to go to Church Stretton to the free school at Burway House which was erected in 1770 on the site of an even earlier school. In 1861 a Public elementary school was opened.

The Hope Bowdler school was built to take 48 children. Exactly how funds were raised to cover the cost of building is not known, but it is obvious that appeals were made beyond the Parish, as a leaflet was circulated in the neighbourhood, seeking contributions.

A BAZAAR
for the sale of
Useful and Fancy Work, Drawings &c
is intended to be held
the 9th and 10th days of August next
at
The Market Hall, Church Stretton
in aid of funds for
Building a School
for the Parish of Hope Bowdler
County of Salop
Your kind support and attendance is requested

Any contributions of Work, Drawings &c for this charitable purpose will be thankfully received by the Rev G J Curtis, Rector at the Rectory Hope Bowdler or (if more convenient) at the Post Office, Church Stretton. July 6th 1854.

Hope Bowdler School, now a private house.

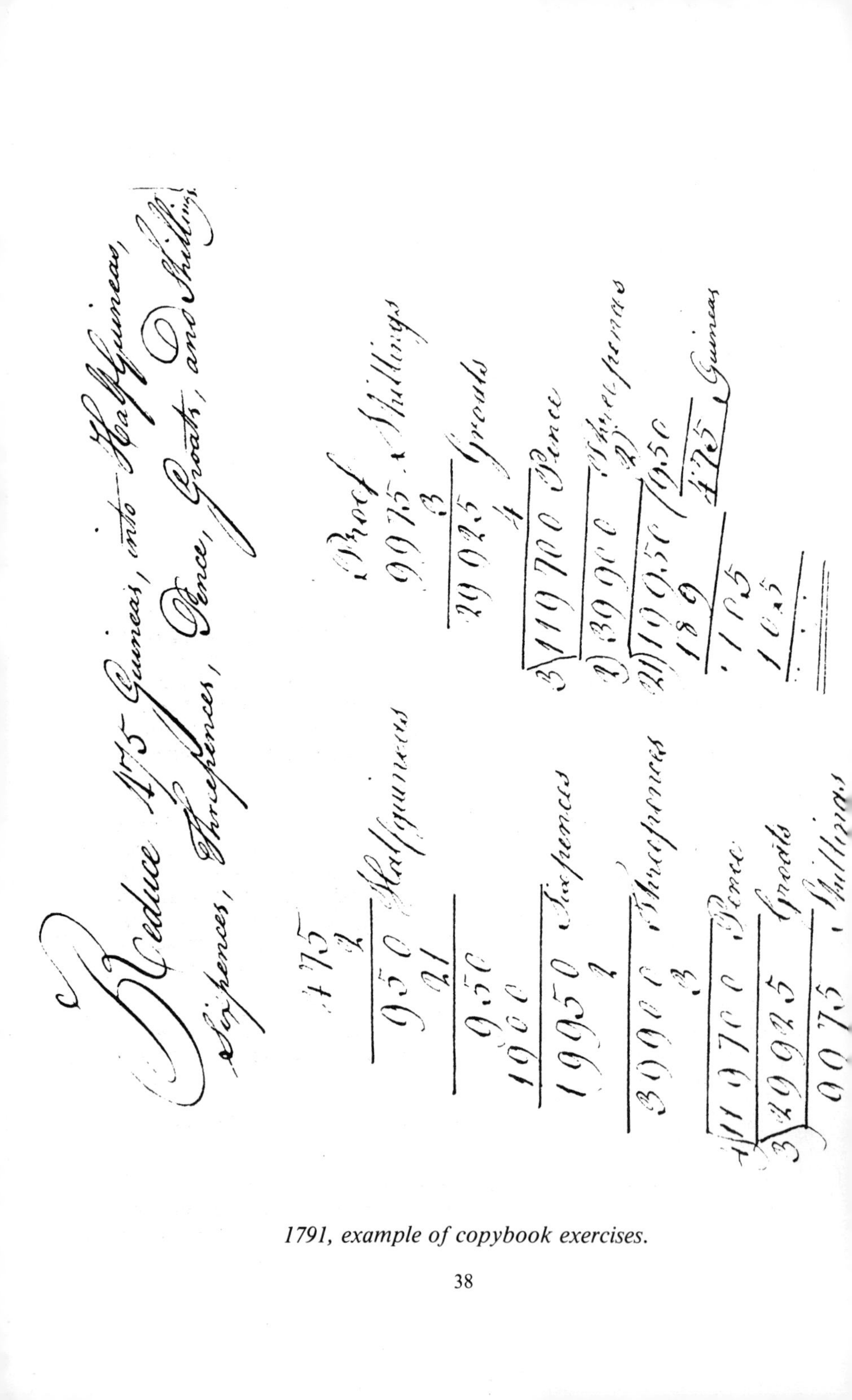

Reduce 475 Guineas, into Halfguineas, Sixpences, Threepences, Pence, Groats, and Shillings.

1791, example of copybook exercises.

HOPE BOWDLER SCHOOL Public Elementary school built in 1856 for 48 children.

1861	Census	
	Jane Abbot	- 21 Schoolmistress
	Jane Poole	- Boarder
1863	Miss Hoy	
1871	Census - called St Andrews National School	
	Ann Rowlands	- 23 Schoolmistress
1881	Census	
	Henry Shenton	- 36 Schoolmaster
	Susannah "	- 33 ass. Mistress d 28/4/85 aged 38
	Ambrose "	- 10 Scholar
1905	Miss Emma Watkins - headmistress.	

The first schoolmistress appears in the census as Jane Abbot, aged 21. Apart from the basic 3 r's, there is no doubt that a lot of time would have been spent copying out existing documents and texts to improve handwriting and, in particular, to perfect the beautiful script that so many people used, especially those whose work involved book-keeping, legal documents and the like. A copy book prepared by John Reynolds in 1791 gives excellent examples of his exercises in arithmetic, calculating areas and costs, etc.

In an earlier chapter the influence of drink in the family is referred to and, as late as the 1890's, it was obviously still common as was noted by a Miss Johnson (later to marry a Croxton) who came to teach at the School and was horrified to find children bringing cider to school to drink with their lunch and then being sleepy during afternoon class. She broke this habit by providing cocoa and soup, often at her own expense, heated on the schoolroom fire.

Another major change that she made was to bring about an end to the custom of 'forelock tugging by the boys and curtseying by the girls' when ever she came into the room, she felt this was outdated. The local 'nobility' did not approve!

The School closed in 1948 when it had an average attendance of 29. It is now a private house.

It is interesting how much of the spelling to be found in letters, bookkeeping accounts and records was phonetic, quite clear in their meaning, but at slight variance with today's usage. Many examples appear in this text from time to time. A representative selection includes:

Jenury (January)
Febury (February)
Gorge (George)
a Count (account)
a Gain (again)
syth (scythe)
shuger (sugar)
currands (currants)
meate (meat)
loyne (loin)
skurt (skirt)
hart (heart)
for quarter (forequarter)

income (income)
chife (chief)
garding (garden)
yurling (yearling)
digen (digging)
rode (road)
rodeman (roadman)
wegges (wedges)

wooll (wool)
peace (piece)
pebles (pebbles)
corne (corn)
tatters (potatoes)
bulocks (bullocks)
coate (coat)
hatt (hat)
monney (money)
surching (searching)
flower (flour)
chees (cheese)
flanel (flannel)
piggs (pigs)
tyling (tiling)
lam (lamb)
lames (lambs)
bords (boards)
Crismus (Christmas)
a Greed (agreed)
leter (letter)
riting (writing)

HOPE BOWLDER CHURCH - ST. ANDREWS

The first record of a church goes back to the 13th century and the first recorded incumbent was Nicholas in 1248. The fully documented registers go back to 1564, the Chalice to 1572 and the pulpit is dated 1639. The church as it stands today was almost entirely rebuilt in 1862, during the time Riou George Benson was the Vicar and his brother, the Lord of the Manor, owning almost the entire village.

Shropshire appears to have been a comparatively poor County until at least the time of Henry VIII, and this is reflected in the large number of Norman churches that have survived in the County, for few communities were ever wealthy enough to rebuild them in a Gothic style.

Before the Church was rebuilt, there was a Gallery at the West end for singers and players. The instruments used were violin, oboe and cello. The floor used to be covered with clean straw every Sunday morning.

The Clergymen and Patrons of the Church were:

1248 Nicholas
1275 Robert de Stapleton
Patron: Sir Eudo de Zouche
1275 Richard Paterike
Sir Eudo de Zouche
1280 William de Bedicote
Dame Millicent de Montalt
1289 John de Chester
Dame Millicent de Montalt
1289 Richard de Bury
Dame Millicent de Montalt
1296 Richard de Heaton
The King as guardian of Philip Brunel's Heir
1303 Alexander de Bokenhale
Sir William de la Zouche
1349 John de Beyston
Sir William de la Zouche
1355 Roger de Chelmedwyke
Sir William de la Zouche
1381 John Marchaunt exchanged with
Henry de Kylpsham
Sir William de la Zouche
Richard Rodde (or Redde) resigned in 1385
1385 Simon Browne exchanged with
Sir William de la Zouche
1386 Roger de Houndeslowe
Sir William de la Zouche
1409 Thomas Checknyll
William Lord Zouche
John Bulhard resigned 1422
1422 John Whytmore
John Earl of Huntingdon
John Smethycote
1435 John Boteler
Lord de la Zouche
Richard Butler died 1508
1508 Maurice Rowland
Lord de la Zouche
Maurice Reede resigned 1523
1523 John Massey
Lord de la Zouche
1564 John Penson
Simon Kemsey
1567 John Price D.C.L.
Simon Kemsey
1569 Edward Threlheld
Simon Kemsey
Peter Scriven (or Scrivener) 1587-1640
1640 Thomas Brompton
Samson Eure

1694 Solomon Tyler
  Richard Davies
1699 Henry Newman
  William Newman
1743 Thomas Pritchard
  Richard Adney, a minor with consent of his Mother, Dorothy Adney
1768 Thomas Warter
  John Stanier of Uppington
1777 John Stanier
  John Stanier
1806 George Watkin Marsh
  Moses George Benson
1852 George James Curtis
  Moses George Benson
1860 Riou George Benson
  Moses George Benson
1896 William Jellicorse
  Ralph B Benson
1905 Arthur Percy Mathews
  Ralph B Benson
1951 John Macwell Philpott
1961 Samuel Charles Robert Lane Clark
1971 Edward Baty
1980 Michael Bromfield

The de la Zouche family do not appear to have had any close connection with the village, but Richard Adney of Ragdon, the Stanier family who owned Ragdon Manor Farm and of course, the Benson family were all closely involved.

The Church, until the establishment of local Government Authorities in the late 19th century, held a very important place in Parish affairs, governing through the agency of the vestry meeting. The Church, and especially the Churchwardens, were involved in secular government.

The strong influence that the Church had on villagers is expressed in the wording of a Will dated 1801 in which it reads:

> "being of perfect mind and memory thanks be given unto God. Therefore calling into mind the Mortality of my Body and knowing that it is appointed for all men to die do make and ordain this my last will and testament that is to say principally and first of all I give and recommend my soul into the hands of Almighty God that gave it and my body I recommend to the Earth to be buried in decent Christian Burial at the Discretion of my Executors nothing doubting but at the General Resurrection I shall receive the same again by the Mighty Power of God and as touching such worldly estate wherewith it had pleased God to bless me in this Life." Then followed the bequests.

There are a large number of the very old grave stones still remaining on the Churchyard, and one of the oldest lies just behind the South Porch and reads:-

"Near this place lie the bodies of Edward Knott and Frances his wife. She died January 12th 1748. He died February 18th 1759 aged 80.

In the quarry where this stone was got
(Edward) mischanced to fall it was his lot
(Time) for preparation it was small
(God) will have mercy on us all
(That) was all that coud be said
(Then in) one minute he was weel and dead

Also Elizabeth, Sarah and Edward son and daughters of Edward Knott and Frances his wife.
Elizabeth d. May 22 1714 aged 2
Sarah d. 21 May 1724 aged 9
Edward d. June 1st 1731 aged 4
also Thomas Knott d. February 2 1752 aged 29"

Nearby is a stone which reads:-

"Here lyeth the body of Richard (Knott)
(?) Knott widow d. 17?? Edward Knott died
Richard Knott died Sarah Knott died"

Note: where the words cannot be deciphered for certain, they are put in brackets.

The Knott family lived at Chelmick during the period given below, then left the parish.

Edward Knott d.18/2/1759 aged 80 - Frances Griffith m.16/6/1711 d.12/1/1748

Elizabeth	Ann	Sarah	Mary	Thomas	Edward
b.27/7/1712	d.20/3/1713	b.24/3/1715	b.6/4/1719	b.25/10/1724	b.4/6/1727
d.22/5/1714		d.21/5/1724		d.2/2/1752	d.1/6/1731

Ann -Ed Thomas m.7/2/1740

Thomas -Margaret

Sarah	Edward	Richard
b.26/6/1749	b.9/12/1750	b.6/12/1752
d.23/2/1823	d.22/7/1816	d.6/4/1823

The Parish registers go back to 1564. In 1661 the records were written in Latin, this change may have been a gesture of joy at the Restoration and the end of the strict Puritan regime. The return to English a few years later was probably due to the unpopularity of Roman Catholicism. The last of the parchment books end in 1779.

There are few references in the records to the requirement of "Burying in Woolen", but there was an Act of Parliament entitled "Act of Burying in Woolen" which was passed in 1678 and stated:

> "No corpse of any person (except those who shall die of the Plague) shall be buried in any shirt, shift, sheet or shroud or anything whatever made or mingled with flax, hemp, silk, hair, gold or silver or in any stuff or thing other than what is made of sheep's wool only or be put in any coffin lined or faced with any material but sheep's wool only."

At the conclusion of the burial service the Clerk asked "who makes affidavit?" This had to be made within 8 days of the funeral. Penalties of £5 were made on the estates of persons not buried in woollen, on the householder in whose house he died, on the persons connected with the funeral, on ministers neglecting to certify non-receipt of the affidavit and on Overseers neglecting to levy the penalty. Half the £5 went to the Poor and half to the informer, so when anyone had decided to defy the Act it was usual for a member of the family to act as informer and so reduce the penalty from £5 to £2 10s 0d.

Parish registers were supposed to have a column for 'The Affid: persons' and one for 'Affidavit certified', but this seems to have ceased after 1684.

The Act was repealed in 1814, and there is reference in Hope Bowdler dated 7th October 1749 - 'I, Elizabeth Speek then made oath that the body of Jane Sankey of the parish of Hope Bowdler was not shrouded or wraped up for Burial in any materials but what was made of sheep's Wool only according to Act of Parliament. Edw. Thomas and Anne Thomas."

John Croxton, who died in 1805 aged 89, had been Clerk to the Parish for 65 years.

The collection of Tithes was organised on a Parochial basis through the Church, and it was not until 1836 that the Tithe Commission was charged with the duty of commuting tithes of produce into rent charges. This work was completed and published in 1843. Today the Tithe maps for the village still exist, but the Tithe Apportionment Manuscript, giving details of the ownership of land, the tenancy, and tithe values, is apparently lost.

The Valuation made in 1843 has been matched to the Tithe records that do exist and is probably an accurate account. It was used in all local tax assessments. The complete record is contained in Appendix 1.

In 1851 the living was calculated to be worth £228. In 1534 it had been £6 13s 4d.

When consideration was being given to rebuild the Church, an estimate was prepared in 1838 which read:

"The estimate of Mason work and material for stripping the back side of Hope Bowdler church and repairing cover on the front side and steeple and witewash the Church outside and inside and mend the plastering outside. The workmen to find tile, lime, sand, lath nailes here and 9ft? of espairing and halling? and Compleat the same in a workmanlike manner for the sum of £16 4s 2d. Josiah Duckett."

As the actual rebuilding was not carried out until 1862, it is likely that this work was either an interim job or never done.

The annual account for 1851 prepared by the Church Wardens, Thos Wilding and John Croxton:

Paid for Partchment		2	0
Paid for postage of a leter			8
2 bottles of wine		10	8
Clerks salary	3	8	0
Bred for Sacrament			4
Paid for Riting the Registers		5	0
Cleaning the Church Yard		1	0
	£4	7	5

In 1853 it was recorded:

Paid for two prop for to loose the Corps in the Graves	2	0
2 planks for the side of the grave	4	8

When the rebuilding was carried out in 1862, Mr. Pontney Smith of Shrewsbury was the designer. Messrs. Nevett of Ironbridge were the contractors. The stone came from Soudley quarries. The total cost was £500 and a Mortgage deed for raising £100 was executed by private bankers at Much Wenlock. The mortgage was signed by four local farmers Philemon Haynes, George Robinson, John Faulkner and Thos. Wilding plus G. Benson, J.P.

At about the same time as this work was being done, Riou George Benson the Vicar had the Vicarage rebuilt and very much enlarged, with the addition of a second floor.

To celebrate the Jubilee of Queen Victoria in 1887 a collection was made for a new, commemorative bell. The amount required was £140 and the records show that a collection of £103 17s 0d from individual contributors from the villagers was made. Nowhere is recorded where the balance came from!

Starlings in the Church were obviously a problem as there is an 1889 entry for "Stopping Starlings in Church 1s 6d."

The Church Walk was made in an effort to improve the approach to the Lych Gate. The blacksmith gave the ironwork, the wheelwright such timbers as were necessary and although no actual record concerning the work involved is to be found, it is probable that this was all done on a voluntary basis.

1887, Church Bell to commemorate the Jubilee of Queen Victoria.

THE 'GHOST HOLE' LEGEND

Just to the front of the old Toll House, in the hillside at the bottom of the hill where the road leads up to Hazler Hill is shown, on the Ordnance map, a "Copper Hole". This was, at one time, mined.

The old Copper Quarry and the 'Ghost Hole' was located behind the wooden building.

However, the hole became notorious, not because of the copper, but because it was believed to be haunted and became known as the "Ghost Hole". To this day the road over Hazler to Ragdon is still called, by some of the older inhabitants, 'Ghost Hole Lane'.

There is no doubt that as recently as the 1930's people were frightened to walk past it at night as it was firmly believed to be haunted, some even claiming to have seen the ghost. As it was the only road from Church Stretton to Hope Bowdler, Soudley and Wall, it was obviously of great concern to the villagers over the years.

Many are the stories told, but the most likely version is that a Sarah Duckett, who lived away from the area, used to come and visit relatives at Soudley and, being friendly with the occupants of the Toll House, used to stop and see them on the way.

On the last occasion that she was seen alive, she had got off the London train, walked up Hazler Road and stopped at the Toll House. She was never seen again and was presumed to have been murdered.

The police were called and, assisted by local people, dug out the old mine shaft, said to be 'as deep as a Church steeple'. Nothing was found that gave any clue, except a woman's shoe - Sarah Duckett's? The police abandoned the search, but local interest persisted and an old woman who lived in the Toll House and reported to be 'off her head' was overheard saying, "I had nothing to do with it, I only held the candle". Was Sarah, as some suggested, buried under the flagstones of the old house? C S Burne in 'Shropshire Folklore 1883' says that she died in a Worcester hospital in 1876. Another report said she had emigrated to Australia and, a letter to Eddowes Shrewsbury Journal September 9th 1881 comments that it was a man returning from a Rent dinner in Church Stretton, doubtless inebriated, who first reported seeing the ghost 'plainly dressed in a cotton bonnet and dress'

So, was Sarah Duckett murdered or did she just disappear? Why the legend of her ghost? A long contemporary poem - 'The Legend of Hazlar' - was published in the 1885 edition of a Handbook of Church Stretton by George R. Windsor and gives a clue in the following extracts:-

"The Church clock struck twelve
A wayfarer strode up the new Hazler Road
He suddenly stops
'Tis a woman's dread ghost standing there by the fence,
That freezes his blood and entrances each sense.
He shook off the horror and walked on with speed
Down the Hope Bowdler road. And having the lead
To outstrip this unearthly strange being he tried,
But still she kept gliding along by his side.
But when he gained courage to have a good look
At his ghostly companion, she then 'took her hook'.

"Why does this poor ghost haunt the roads in the night?
Does she know of some treasure she wants brought to light?
Suppose she was murdered? Oh! horrible thought
And to stern justice wants her foul murderer brought"

"A wandering maiden, Miss Duckett by name,
Who by movements erratic was well known to fame,
Was seen, years before, on the Hazler highway
And had never been heard of, or seen since that day;
She had been just before, of her father bereaved,
He had left her some money, and it was believed,
She had then on her person the cash she received."

"Near the place where the ghost had our hero apalled,
Is a disused mine shaft, the Old Copper Hole called,
And 'twas Miss Duckett's tomb almost every one fears"

"They murdered poor Sarah, we know that they didden,
And her body is in that Old Copper Hole hidden".

They said the shaft must be emptied, the remains of the poor murdered girl found and buried in hallowed ground. Men volunteered to work, farmers promised victuals and beer, some started a subscription to aid. They work early and late "Like horses they work in the damp narrow hole". The story is reported in all England's newspapers - 'The Copper Hole Ghost'.

One day they found an old shoe - "This article gave them encouragement great in the work of discovering Sarah's sad fate".

"But when at the shaft's bottom they stand on hard ground
And no vestige of Miss Duckett's bones have they found."
Had she died far distant from the old Copper Hole?

There was, in 1861, a 19 year old Dairymaid called Sarah Duckett living and working at Upper Farm, Chelmick. Was it she who went away to live and work and who, upon returning to see her relations at Soudley, disappeared?

The fears of the villagers were such that few would ever walk alone past the Ghost Hole at night, and as late as 1932 to one child, Ron Wilkes of Wall Bank, his fear plus his imagination sent him racing back down Sandford Avenue to the safety and comfort of street lights and houses. He tells how, going home one evening on his bicycle, just after it had got dark, that he had made himself press on up the road and not be frightened to go past the Ghost Hole but, as he got to the brow of the hill he stopped, trying to muster up the courage necessary to go on when he heard the 'click', 'click', 'click' of footsteps coming down off Hazler Hill. He stood paralysed and through the darkness from the direction of the sounds, there appeared a white ghostly figure. That was too much for Ron who turned his bicycle round and flew back down the hill, not stopping until he reached the bottom where, shivering and shakiing he tried to compose himself. After a few minutes he heard the footsteps again, getting nearer and nearer until the figure came out into the lamplight. It was a man who had been playing cricket, still in his whites and cricket boots, who had been out for an evening walk - so much for the ghost, but young Ron Wilkes went back to his Uncle's home, nothing would have got him to go past the Ghost Hole that night!

The 'Ghost' was, for years, a talking point among the people and pubs of Church Stretton, as well as the villagers up the Wenlock road. No doubt being exaggerated with each telling. One night, after an evening in one of the many Stretton pubs, Mr. Marsh - a shoemaker -

and his son were walking back home to Wall. There had been a lot of talk of the 'Ghost' that evening, and as they got near the top of Sandford Avenue, a ghostly figure draped in a sheet appeared. Mr. Marsh, without more ado, set about the 'ghost' with his heavy ended stick. Next day everyone knew the identity of the 'ghost', he was walking around Stretton with a black eye and a cut forehead - he was Steve Hotchkiss - and that may have been the last time the ghost was ever seen!

Today, nobody fears to pass the old Ghost Hole that had for so many years terrified the local people. Is the spirit of Sarah Duckett still there, waiting to be released? In any case she must have been a friendly spirit as there are no tales of anyone ever being harmed, just scared out of their wits!

THE STORY OF JANE MORRIS

There were strict laws concerning the 'Poor' at this time, and the case of Jane Morris gives an interesting example of how the law was carried out in the case of an illegitimate child.

The Church has numerous entries of the baptism of base, natural or bastard children and most of these were, in one way or another, accepted into village life without fuss or bother, many later marrying and becoming part of the community. Some, however, became a charge on the Parish and came under the Overseers of the Poor.

The case of Jane Morris is fully documented and while it certainly involved a lot of time for the Justices of the Peace and other authorities, it does give an idea of life and the law at that period.

Jane Morris was a single girl, but how she came to be in Hope Bowdler, where she lived or worked and who her parents were is not known. She was probably a girl of little education, as any documents in this case shown to have been signed by her were with her mark XX.

There is little doubt that her pregnancy came about as result of the Stretton May Fair jollifications in May 1755. The father was John Harrington, born May 23rd 1736 of Richard and Anne Harrington, a tailor of Church Stretton.

Thus far there is very little different in this story from many others, yet it follows a bizarre sequence of events and hearings before the Justices of the Peace and Churchwardens of two counties that is difficult to understand. These are the facts taken from the official records and documents.

1755 15th Day of December "ORDER TO REMOVE A PERSON"
(by this time Jane Morris was seven months pregnant)

A complaint made by the Churchwardens and Overseers of the Poor of "ye parish of Leintwardine on ye north side of ye water in ye county of Hereford" that "Jane Morris, single woman big with child hath lately intruded herself into the said parish of Leintwardine, thear to inhabit as a parishioner contrary to the laws relating to settlements of the poor."

It is clear that up to this time she had been living in Hope Bowdler.

Two of His Majesties (George II) Justices of the Peace, one being of the Quorum for the County of Hereford did upon "Due Examination and Enquiry made into the premisses upon the Oath of the said Jane Morris" adjudge that she was likely to become chargeable on the Parish of Leintwardine. As a result, in His Majesty's name, it was ordered that she be "forthwith removed and conveyed from the Parish of Leintwardine to the Parish of Hope Bowdler, and her deliver to the Churchwardens and Overseers of the Poor" and "they are likewise required in His Majesties' name to receive the said Jane Morris and provide for her, their own Parishioner."

Where she was lodged and what sort of Christmas she would have had is not known, but what is known is that on 27th December 1755 on Examination on Oath, before Tho. More and Edward Perks:-

> "saith she is now with child which when born will be a Bastard and may be chargeable to the Parish whear born and she further saith that John Harrington of Church Stretton in the month of May last seduced her to permit him to have carnal knowledge of her Body and that he is the Father of the said child, no one but he ever had carnal knowledge of her Body."

It would be reasonable to assume that she was an ignorant, harmless and probably friendless girl - running away to Leintwardine tends to indicate this - yet there she is, just two weeks after being brought back to Hope Bowdler, having to undergo a verbal examination and admit to two strange men the intimate details of her seduction, which had probably occurred at the end of a gay and happy day at the May Fair.

On the same day, December 27th, John Croxton who was Clerk to the Parish in Hope Bowdler was, together with all the High and Petty Constables in the County of Salop, sworn to execute the warrant:

> "to bring the said John Harrington before me (Tho. More) if you can apprehend him in your duties that such order may be taken with him as the Law directs and hearof fail not at your peril given under my hand and seal the year and day above written. T More."

No doubt John Harrington duly appeared before Mr. More to his satisfaction and the case was temporarily suspended.

Meanwhile, a boy was born on 20th February 1756, duly baptised and entered in the Church records. But that was by no means the end of the matter and it appears that the Harrington family, while protesting the innocence of their son John, were not without some influence, because young Jane Morris was once again brought before two Justices of the Peace, Revd. Thomas Salwey L.L.O. and Francis Walker Esq. for a further Examination upon Oath on 8th April 1756.

This Examination produced a further admission from Jane that she had not given to Tho. More in the previous December. The record shows that:

> "This examinant saith sometime in the Middle of Month of May 1755 one John Harrington, Yeoman, through persuasions had carnal knowledge of the examinant's Body and shee having Aquaintance afterwards with one Thomas Baylis he also had carnal knowledge of the examinant's Body on or about the 15th Day of June 1755 and she further saith that on the 20th Day of February 1756 she was delivered of a Male Bastard Child in the Parish of Hope Bowdler and that the child was come to his full growth and also saith that she believes the said John Harrington is the Father.
> Sworn before us Thomas Salwey and Francis Walker. XX the mark of Jane Morris."

So, the baby was born, she had admitted a second 'affair' and although John Harrington had not yet admitted being the father, it might appear, once again, that that was that. Not at all, on the same day, 8th April, Messrs. Salwey and Walker took further drastic action, or so it would appear.

> "Following her Examination and a Complaint by the Churchwardens of Hope Bowdler that her child had been chargeable to the Parish since its birth and would continue to be so, the two Justices of the Peace in the name of His Majesty King George the Second commanded the Petty Constable of Hope Bowdler 'to convey ye said Jane Morris from your sd Township of Hope Bowdler to ye House of Correction at Salop and deliver her to the Master thereof and you the sd Master of ye sd House of Correction are hereby required to receive the sd Jane Morris into your sd house and her safely keep to hard labour for one whole year ... fail not at your perils."

(The House of Correction was properly known as the County Bridewell and was a building adjoining the Gaol, with which it had communication. The prisoners therein were allowed to attend upon Divine Service in the County Gaol. The Master was probably Mr. Price Micklestone, a saddler, or John Baugh, who had a salary of £50.)

Why such punishment? Surely there was nothing so sinister about her downfall.

However, in the 17th Century, because bastard children were likely to become paupers, penalties for their parents could be severe. Fathers went to Gaol until they found security for the child's maintenance and Mothers to the House of Correction for a year. So, it appears a century later, the same punishment was meted out on Jane Morris.

As well as being Petty Constable, John Croxton was also the local carrier, and these notes from his account book are obviously linked to the case.

"For going to Stretton to take Jn Harrington and taking him to Ludlow. Spent at Stretton on the rode and at Ludlow	6s 10d
For taking John Harrington to Ludlow	1s 6d
For taking Jane Morris to Salop and bringing her home	4s 0d
Spent at Shrewsbury for the horses and ourselves	11s 5d

RECOGNIZANCE

"Be it remembered on the twenty ninth day of May 1756 John Harrington, Taylor and Richard Harrington also a Taylor of the Parish of Church Stretton came before me Thos. Salwey and acknowledged themselves to owe our Sovereign Lord the King, viz John Harrington Thirty pounds and Richard Harrington Twenty pounds to be levied on their respective goods

and chattels, lands and tenements for the use of His Majesty His Heirs and Successors if default be made in the conditions underwritten.
"The Condition of this Recognizance is such that whereas a male Bastard Child was lately born of the Body of Jane Morris in the Parish of Hope Bowdler, aforesaid single woman with child is now chargeable to the sd parish and whereas the sd Jane Morris hath upon her Oath charged John Harrington aforesaid to be the true and only Father of the sd child.
"If therefore the above bounden John and Richard Harrington do and shall appear at the next General Quarter Sessions of the Peace to be holden at Salop and the sd John Harrington shall then and their abide and receive what shall be enjoined by ye sd Court concerning the premisses aforesaid then this Recognizance to be void or else to Remain in full force."

But now, four months after the baby was born, John Harrington took it upon himself to give notice to Churchwardens and Overseers of the Poor in Hope Bowdler that he would at the Quarter Sessions referred to in the Recognizance of 29th May appear against the Order adjudging him to be the reputed father, dated 5th day of June.

The record of the Quarter Sessions is not available, but John Harrington must have lost because "John Walcot and Godolphin Edwards Esquires late of His Majesties Justices of the Peace on the fourteenth day of July in the Thirtieth year of the reign (1756) of his Majesty King George the Second duly ruled that the said male Bastard child is become chargeable on the said Parish of Hope Bowdler and that John Harrington did beget the said Bastard child and whereas the said John Harrington hath appeared before us and hath not shewn any sufficient cause why he shall not be the reputed father. We do order as well for the better relief of the said Parish of Hope Bowdler as for the sustenation of the said bastard that the said John Harrington shall pay or cause to be paid the sum of five pounds ten shillings and eight pence towards the lying in and he shall likewise pay the sum of one shilling weekly towards the keeping and sustenance and maintenance for and during so long as the said bastard child shall be chargeable to the Parish and we do further order that the said Jane Morris shall also pay sixpence a week in case she shall not nurse and take care of the said child herself."

In the Leebotwood register for June 29 1780 the baptism of Charlotte, base child of Jane Morris is recorded. The same Jane Morris?

HOUSES

In the early Middle Ages life in this Welsh border region was unsettled and inhabitants would not have put much effort into building permanent houses. From the time of Domesday and throughout the time of the Welsh feuding and raiding, it is evident that villages in this area had been laid waste from time to time.

Although after Edward's subjugation of Wales conditions became more settled, there are no houses in the Parish dating back to the 14th century and, in any case, the area was suffering acute economic distress and any elaborate domestic building was unlikely.

The first evidence of any recovery and boom for agriculture - sheep and wool - came in Elizabethan times, there being so many Elizabethan farm houses in the area and, with no credit available in those days, their building must have been preceded by some prosperity.

The houses were half-timbered or entirely stone built and would have housed farm workers as well as the family. They were of moderate size and were still being used in this way up to the end of the 19th century.

In the 'History of Myddle' it states that the first labourers' cottages were built around 1580 and the first recorded example was at Kenly, 10 miles South of Shrewsbury.

The Terms of the 1589 Act for Cottages laid down that "new cottages should have at least 4 acres of land attached to them". It is doubtful if this was ever generally enforced - it had been 2 acres previously. The reasoning behind the Act was probably because of the low wages of agicultural workers and their need to supplement income by the profits of a smallholding where they could grow some corn, perhaps more than they needed, plus keeping a few animals for their household wants.

Although there are early records of individual houses, it was only following the census in 1841 that a reasonably accurate picture of the houses and their occupants can be built up. In some cases, the ages in the earlier census can be as much as 5-10 years out, and only by studying Church records can exact ages be determined. It is not possible to make direct comparisons with this century, as census details remain - by law - secret for 100 years, so in the table overleaf the 1984 statistics are taken from the electoral roll and the children under 18 by an actual head count.

The population count illustrates the change in the number of people living in each house and, of course, most of the 19th century houses were smaller than the average today.

Parish of Hope Bowlder - POPULATION - Adults & children

YEAR	*NUMBER*	*OCCUPIED HOUSES*	*AVERAGE PER HOUSE*
1801	130		
1811	172		
1821	179		
1831	202		
1841	184	30	6.1
1851	169	28	6.0
1861	178	28	6.4
1871	197	32	6.2
1881	163	28	5.8
1891	156		
1901	132		
1911	144		
1921	121		
1931	142		
1951	170		
1961	181		
1984	168	63	2.7

Breaking down the occupants for 1881 and 1984 into adults and children, the change in the pattern is dramatic, with an average of 3 children per house in 1881 compared with 0.5 or ½ a child today.

YEAR	*OCCUPIED HOUSES*	*UNIN-HABITED*	*TOTAL*	*AGE*	*M*	*F*	*TOTAL*
1881							
HOPE BOWLDER	15	2	17	18+	19	17	36
				18−	22	33	55
CHELMICK	11	4	15	18+	16	8	24
				18 -	9	14	23
RAGDON	2	0	2	18+	15	5	20
				18−	2	3	5
							163
1984							
HOPE BOWLDER	44	0	44	18+	50	44	94
				18−	9	8	17
CHELMICK	13	1	14	18+	13	15	28
				18−	5	6	11
RAGDON	6	0	6	18+	7	8	15
				18−	2	1	3
							168

Hope Bowdler Parish boundary remained unaltered until 1968 when Dryhill Farm (24 acres) on the South East side of the Ragleth Hill was included and then, in 1986, the boundary line through Soudley was altered to include Stonehouse Farm.

In 1841 the Hope Bowdler Estate (which did not include Chelmick or Ragdon) was owned by Moses George Benson who, although Lord of the Manor, did not live in the Parish, residing at Lutwyche Hall. The Estate included all the farms and houses in the village apart from Croxton's blacksmith house and forge, which had been given to him in 1759 by William Lutwyche who then owned the Estate, and two cottages along the Soudley Road (Tithe 113/4) (earlier referred to as belonging to the widow Gough), owned by John Broom.

With the number of houses remaining more or less constant throughout the 19th century, much can be gleaned about the population, although the information was basic, from the census returns. No locations of dwellings were given, but with the village being so small this was not really necessary.

Further information can normally be obtained from the Tithe Maps and Tithe Apportionment manuscripts which were prepared in 1843 when the payment of tithes by produce was replaced by payment against 'rent value' for every property and piece of land. The preparation of the Tithe maps which showed every field name and number, and the Manuscript which detailed acreages, rods, perches, rent value, owner and tenant, was without doubt the most accurate record available since the Domesday Book in 1086. Unfortunately, despite searches of the County Archives and the Church records, I can find no copy of the Tithe Apportionment manuscript. The Tithe maps are still available and from these and certain records of Wm Wyley of Wellington dated 9th March 1843, I have been able to establish (and record) the Apportionment details. I have also listed the 18th Century field numbers and matched them to the Tithe details. See Appendix 1.

CROXTON

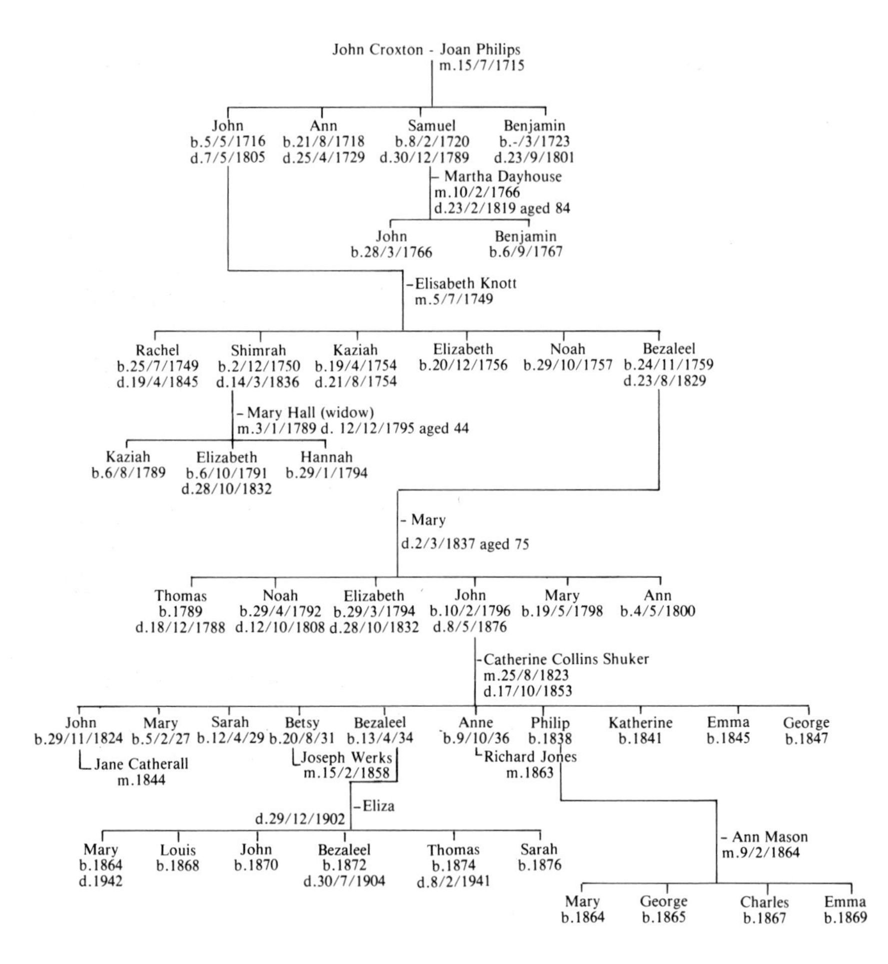

John Croxton - Joan Philips
m.15/7/1715
John
b.5/5/1716
d.7/5/1805
Ann
b.21/8/1718
d.25/4/1729
Samuel
b.8/2/1720
d.30/12/1789
Benjamin
b.-/3/1723
d.23/9/1801
- Martha Dayhouse
m.10/2/1766
d.23/2/1819 aged 84
John
b.28/3/1766
Benjamin
b.6/9/1767
-Elisabeth Knott
m.5/7/1749
Rachel
b.25/7/1749
d.19/4/1845
Shimrah
b.2/12/1750
d.14/3/1836
Kaziah
b.19/4/1754
d.21/8/1754
Elizabeth
b.20/12/1756
Noah
b.29/10/1757
Bezaleel
b.24/11/1759
d.23/8/1829
- Mary Hall (widow)
m.3/1/1789 d. 12/12/1795 aged 44
Kaziah
b.6/8/1789
Elizabeth
b.6/10/1791
d.28/10/1832
Hannah
b.29/1/1794
- Mary
d.2/3/1837 aged 75
Thomas
b.1789
d.18/12/1788
Noah
b.29/4/1792
d.12/10/1808
Elizabeth
b.29/3/1794
d.28/10/1832
John
b.10/2/1796
d.8/5/1876
Mary
b.19/5/1798
Ann
b.4/5/1800
-Catherine Collins Shuker
m.25/8/1823
d.17/10/1853
John
b.29/11/1824
Mary
b.5/2/27
Sarah
b.12/4/29
Betsy
b.20/8/31
Bezaleel
b.13/4/34
Anne
b.9/10/36
Philip
b.1838
Katherine
b.1841
Emma
b.1845
George
b.1847
Jane Catherall
m.1844
Joseph Werks
m.15/2/1858
Richard Jones
m.1863
-Eliza
d.29/12/1902
Mary
b.1864
d.1942
Louis
b.1868
John
b.1870
Bezaleel
b.1872
d.30/7/1904
Thomas
b.1874
d.8/2/1941
Sarah
b.1876
- Ann Mason
m.9/2/1864
Mary
b.1864
George
b.1865
Charles
b.1867
Emma
b.1869

SOME OLD FAMILIES

The details in the Census returns from 1841 to 1881 give a comprehensive picture of the population in each of the years that the census was carried out, but cannot be considered as a complete record of all the people who lived in the Parish in the 19th century. However they do give some interesting information.

The average population - adults and children - was 178. It has sometimes been said that in those days a large number of children died at a very early age and people did not live to be very old, Hope Bowdler certainly contradicts these assumptions.

If we look at all those who had lived to be 60 or older, we find that farmers lived to an average age of 72, their wives and other women in the village, lived an average of a year older to 73, and agricultural labourers and other workers averaged 74 on their death. It appears that although life was hard, amenities lacking - certainly by today's standards - and medical care nowhere near as readily available as now, they lived to ripe old ages, several well into their 90's.

A number of families lived in the Parish for most of the 1800's, very often in the same house. However there were very few, certainly through the male line, still there after the early 1900's.

HOPE BOWDLER

In Hope Bowdler the Croxton family went back to at least 1715 when John and Joan Philips were married, and they were blacksmiths without a break until Thomas died in 1941. (see family tree).

The Hammonds and Jones - wheelwrights - both stayed until 1921 when the Estate was sold up.

The Preece family did not come to the village until 1897 when George P. Preece (son of George Preece the nurseryman in Church Stretton who was involved with the building of Sandford Avenue) was tenant of Upper House Farm and, later, Lower House Farm too. In 1921 he purchased both these farms and Manor Farm, and his three sons George, Frank and Billy farmed them. Today, George F. W. Preece lives just out of the Parish but still farms the Upper House and Manor Farm land.

Although only one of the Benson family ever lived in the Parish, they influenced village life for nearly 100 years.

Moses Benson came to Lutwyche from Liverpool where he had been a shipper, and very much involved in the African trade. He had been very successful and made a lot of money, enabling him to buy Lutwyche Hall and the Lutwyche Estate, following the death of William Lutwyche, with lands and property involving thousands of acres in Shropshire. Moses died in 1806 and was succeeded by his eldest son Captain Ralph who, after his death in 1845, was succeeded by his eldest son Moses George, who had married Charlotte Browne. He adopted his role of Squire with enthusiasm, rebuilding Lutwyche Hall and acquiring the Hope Bowdler Estate from the late W Cheney Hart, in 1828.

Moses George's son, Ralph Augustus, was nominated as Landowner of the Hope Bowdler Estate in 1843 when the Tithe Apportionment details were finalised. The only member of the Benson family to live in the Parish was Riou George, as Rector, and his twelfth child, John Ingham, died aged 86 and was buried in Hope Bowdler churchyard in 1966, and his son the Rev George Riou, now retired, lives in All Stretton.

Rev Riou George and Mary Benson and their 13 children outside the Rectory, 1884.

Another son of Ralph Augustus, Ralph Beaumont (after whom Beaumont Road in Church Stretton was named) married Caroline Essex Cholmondeley (after whom Essex Road was named) then ran the Estate. His son George, sold the Hope Bowdler Estate in 1921 to pay death duties. All the remaining Benson lands were sold shortly after the last war.

RAGDON

In Ragdon the Wilding family have certainly farmed Ragdon Farm since the late 1700's. There were also two other branches of the same family who were influential in the area. Dr. William Wilding, his son and grandson, were all doctors or 'surgeons' (as they were at one time known) practising in Church Stretton and, together, covered more than 100 years. Much of the time they lived at 17 High Street. The others were those connected with the Church, Vicar of Easthope etc., and lived at All Stretton owning much of the land there in the 18th and 19th centuries.

The Ragdon family has a quite clear line back from today to the marriage of Richard Wilding of Bethcote and Mary Watters of Pulverbatch (see family tree) in 1726. Thus seven generations back is definite from young Thomas born 5th March 1986 to Richard and Suzanne Wilding. To go back further is supposition, but based on a process of elimination (and some guesswork!) I think it is likely that 'John Wyldinge and Alice Prees of Ludlow' married in 1630, through their son Richard who married Margaret Todd in 1667, are the 10th generation back. I can find no record (as yet) of any children of Richard and Margaret who could be the link to Richard and Mary but, around this time in the Smethcott parish church records, it states for some entries "taken from Mr. Wilding's book at Bethcote". Perhaps the family fell out with the church or became non-conformist for a period - we may never know.

Nevertheless, with an Alice Wilding coming to Ragdon Farm as a bride in 1680 and the known 13th century association, the family have the longest link with the Parish of any family.

The Church records show several people as being 'of Ragdon' but, unfortunately, it was not common practice to identify locations in the register entries. These include the Adney family who most probably lived at Ragdon Manor Farm in the late 1600's. The register of Baptisms records that Richard and Dorothy Adney had five children between 1725 and 1740. Their third child, Richard, became Patron of the Church when still a minor in 1743 and continued to hold this position until 1768. He married Letitia Oney on March 1st 1752, by which time he had himself entered the church and was a reverend. In 1734 it is recorded that "Tabitha, bastard daughter of Susanna Hanbury, Father'd upon Richard Adney, was baptised 7th April".

WILDING

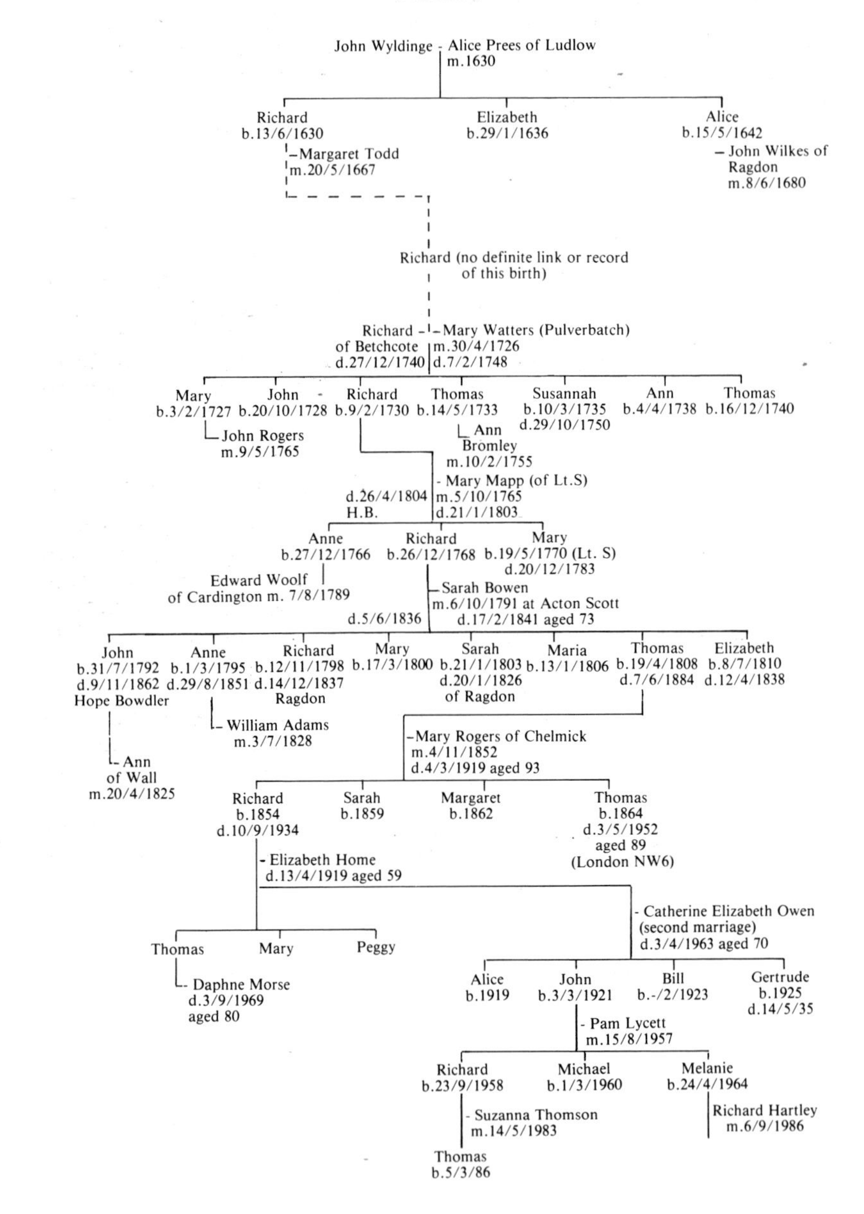

John Wyldinge - Alice Prees of Ludlow
m.1630
Richard
b.13/6/1630
-Margaret Todd
m.20/5/1667
Elizabeth
b.29/1/1636
Alice
b.15/5/1642
- John Wilkes of
Ragdon
m.8/6/1680
Richard (no definite link or record
of this birth)
Richard -
of Betchcote
d.27/12/1740
-Mary Watters (Pulverbatch)
m.30/4/1726
d.7/2/1748
Mary
b.3/2/1727
John Rogers
m.9/5/1765
John
b.20/10/1728
Richard
b.9/2/1730
Thomas
b.14/5/1733
Ann
Bromley
m.10/2/1755
Susannah
b.10/3/1735
d.29/10/1750
Ann
b.4/4/1738
Thomas
b.16/12/1740
- Mary Mapp (of Lt.S)
d.26/4/1804
H.B.
m.5/10/1765
d.21/1/1803
Anne
b.27/12/1766
Edward Woolf
of Cardington m. 7/8/1789
Richard
b.26/12/1768
-Sarah Bowen
m.6/10/1791 at Acton Scott
d.5/6/1836
d.17/2/1841 aged 73
Mary
b.19/5/1770 (Lt. S)
d.20/12/1783
John
b.31/7/1792
d.9/11/1862
Hope Bowdler
- Ann
of Wall
m.20/4/1825
Anne
b.1/3/1795
d.29/8/1851
- William Adams
m.3/7/1828
Richard
b.12/11/1798
d.14/12/1837
Ragdon
Mary
b.17/3/1800
Sarah
b.21/1/1803
d.20/1/1826
of Ragdon
Maria
b.13/1/1806
Thomas
b.19/4/1808
d.7/6/1884
Elizabeth
b.8/7/1810
d.12/4/1838
-Mary Rogers of Chelmick
m.4/11/1852
d.4/3/1919 aged 93
Richard
b.1854
d.10/9/1934
- Elizabeth Home
d.13/4/1919 aged 59
Sarah
b.1859
Margaret
b.1862
Thomas
b.1864
d.3/5/1952
aged 89
(London NW6)
- Catherine Elizabeth Owen
(second marriage)
d.3/4/1963 aged 70
Thomas
- Daphne Morse
d.3/9/1969
aged 80
Mary
Peggy
Alice
b.1919
John
b.3/3/1921
- Pam Lycett
m.15/8/1957
Bill
b.-/2/1923
Gertrude
b.1925
d.14/5/35
Richard
b.23/9/1958
- Suzanna Thomson
m.14/5/1983
Thomas
b.5/3/86
Michael
b.1/3/1960
Melanie
b.24/4/1964
Richard Hartley
m.6/9/1986

This appears to have been accepted quite openly and he and Dorothy had two more children before his death in 1739. Who Susanna Hanbury was is not known, neither she nor her family appear in any local records, so it is a possibility that she was a servant. Tabitha must have continued to live in the village, because it is almost certainly she who was the 19 year old bride of Josiah Duckett married at Hope Bowdler on October 19th 1752 - they had four children.

CHELMICK

At the time of the Herald's Visitation in 1623, it listed the family name through fifteen generations as Chelmudewyk, Chelmundwyk, Chelmedwick, Chelmewyke and Chelmick. The heir was given as "Tho. Chelmick de Chelmick et de Ragdon in Co. Salop". He was one of four brothers and after Henry's burial on 4th July 1633, their name does not appear again in the Hope Bowdler Church register. In fact, the family appear to have left Chelmick in 1635 and the two farms (Upper and Chelmick Manor) were sold. An Indenture between Thomas and Frances Chelmick and Viscount Lumley was signed for four messuages or tenements in Chelmick.

Descendants of Thomas Chelmick are still living in Shrewsbury.

The Jones family at Chelmick Pools were originally at the Cwms Farm where Thomas Jones farmed. His two sons Edward and Richard worked with him for several years, then they went as lodgers at Dryhill Farm, where they were working as woodsmen. Richard then married and moved to Chelmick Pools where he and his wife Ann had eight children.

As has been said elsewhere Richard, together with his sons Philemon and Jasper, farmed, worked in timber and carried on contract farm work in the area. Jasper built a small house above the family home in the 1930's. His son, Norman, still lives in a house built on the site of his grandfather's house where, for many years before and after the last war, two of Jasper's sisters ran very successful tea rooms. In 1956, when both in their 80's, they retired.

1913, the Golden Wedding of Richard and Ann Jones. (l. to r. back row) Mary Ellen, Fanny and Emma. (second row) Philemon, Clara, Sarah, Katherine and Jasper. Fanny and Sarah ran the Tea Rooms.

HOPE BOWDLER - PEOPLE AND HOUSES

It has been possible to identify nearly every 18th and 19th century house and plot them on the map overleaf. A few houses can be traced back even further.

Taking the 1841 census as the starting point, a visitor would have found the following picture, first going to Hope Bowdler village and then, later, on to Chelmick and Ragdon.

Assuming he took either the old Hazler Road out of Church Stretton towards Much Wenlock or the road from All Stretton across the Leasowes, he would have arrived at the Turnpike or Toll House.

The Toll House was situated near the two white posts. The New Road - Sandford Avenue - on the right, the old Hazler Road opposite and the track up to Hazler Hill and Ragdon on the left.

This was also known as the Hazler Gate. Tolls were collected for all horse drawn vehicles, flocks of sheep, etc. until around 1870. The coming of the railway in 1860 brought about the end of the toll charge system.

CHURCH STRETTON
STRETTON
Hazler
3
Gaudford Seat
Pluoks Coppice
Hazler Hill
Gough's Coppice
Overdale
Wood
4
Hazler Barn
Spring
21
A
Dryhill
The Mount
Tanks
HOPE BOWL
Rayleth Hill
1000
900
800
Nether Springs
26
20
Ragdon
21
24
25
Chelmick
22/3
Little Coppice

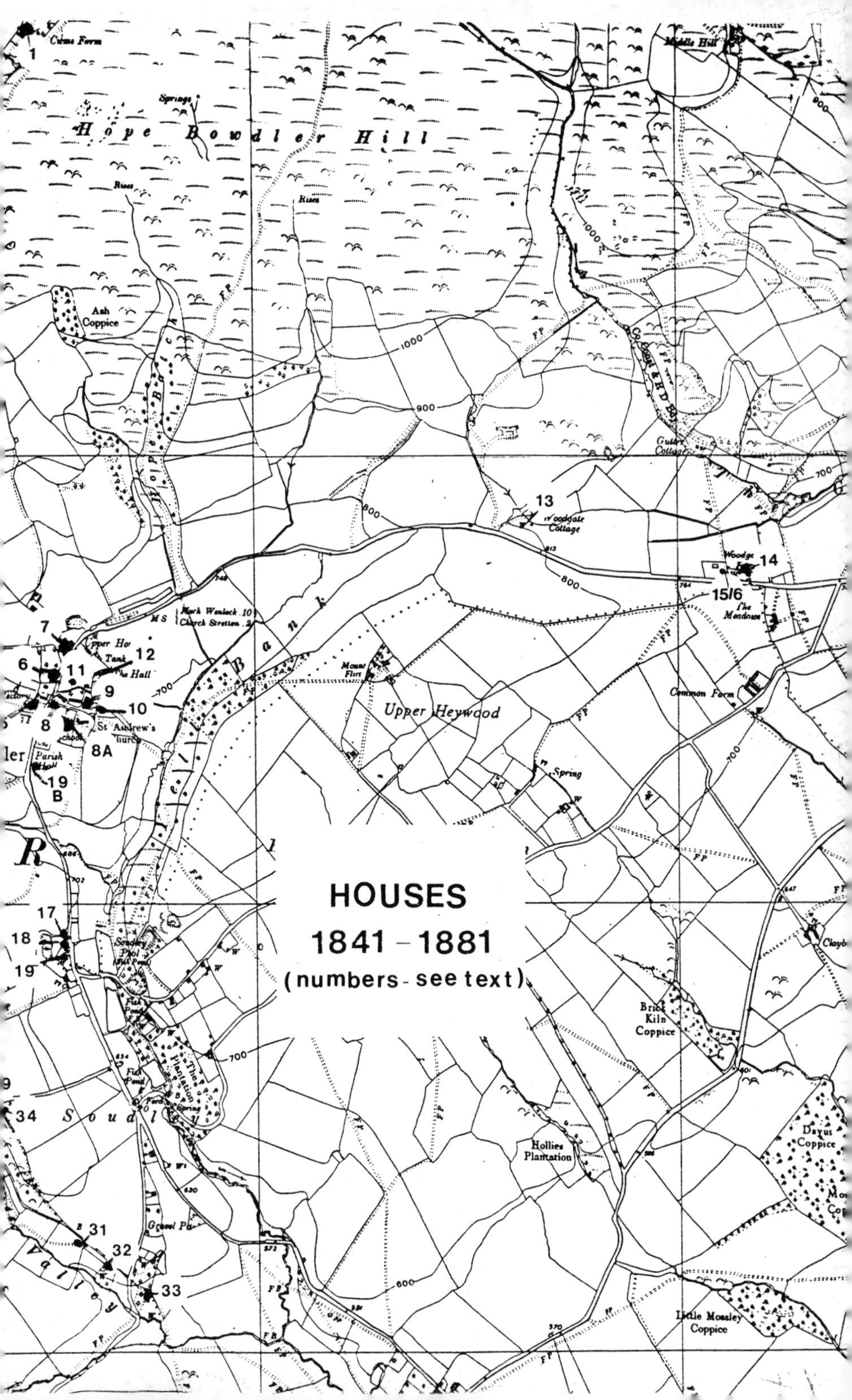
HOUSES
1841 - 1881
(numbers - see text)
Hope Bowdler Hill
Ash Coppice
Upper Heywood
Woodgate Cottage
St Andrew's Church
Parish Hall
Common Farm
Brick Kiln Coppice
Hollies Plantation
Dayus Coppice
Little Mossley Coppice
Gutter Cottage
Middle Hill
Mount Flirt
Soudley
Valley
The Plantation
Much Wenlock 10
Church Stretton 2
1
7
6
11
12
9
10
8
8A
19
B
13
14
15/6
17
18
19
34
31
32
33

In 1838 John Sankey probably lived there, then came John Morgan who, with his wife Ann, brought up 6 children there. He is listed as being an Agricultural labourer, so it is likely that his wife collected the tolls when he was at work. There would not have been very much traffic in those days.

In 1861 William Merrick and his wife Ann were living there and he was recorded as being a 'Collector of Tolls'. Perhaps with the building of the railway, traffic increased to require the full-time services of a Collector.

In 1871 Richard Corfield, also an agricultural labourer, lived there. There is no further reference to this property which was rated at £2 2s 0d a year with a rental of £2 10s 0d.

HAZLER GATE - TOLL HOUSE - MAP No. 3.
Part of Hope Bowlder Estate bought by Moses George Benson.

1841 Census
John Morgan - 30 Agric. Lab.
Ann ,, - 29
Hannah ,, - 2
John ,, - 8 mths

1843 Valuation. Estimated Rental £2-10-0. Rateable value £2-2-0

1851 Census
John Morgan - 42 Agric. Lab.
Ann ,, - 40
Hannah ,, - 12
John ,, - 10
William ,, - 9
Edwin ,, - 6
Thomas ,, - 2
Edward ,, - 7 mths

1861 Census
William Merrick - 44 Collector of Tolls
Ann ,, - 48

1871 Census
Richard Corfield - 45 Agric. Lab.
Elizabeth ,, - 35
Emma ,, - 6
Thomas ,, - 4
John ,, - 2

No further reference to this property, but it was knocked down when the new road was built.

The new road, Sandford Avenue, was named after the rector of Eaton-upon-Heywood, the Rev. Holland Sandford who, with local men of influence, formed a committee to build the road and plant an avenue of lime trees, the first being planted at a Ceremony on 19th December 1884, when George Preece, nurseryman, handed the Rev. Sandford a spade with which he planted the first tree. The individual trees were all 'sponsored' by local dignateries, business men and farmers, and one was planted in the name of the Prince of Wales. In 1886 Queen Victoria was 'graciously pleased to assent to name 2 trees - Queen Victoria's tree and Prince Consort's tree.' The Avenue extended from the centre of the town up the Wenlock road to the Turnpike.

At Hazler Gate, the Turnpike, a left turn up a lane towards the Gaer Stone, between Helmeth and Hope Bowdler Hills, lead to Cwms Farm and at the top of the hill just before the farm was a small cottage and garden described in the Sale details of 1819 as 'patch open to the road'. In 1841 Samuel and Mary Bowen lived there until he died in 1849 aged 65. The rent was 15s a year and, as no further record appears, it most probably became derelict after his death.

COTTAGE AND GARDEN - MAP No. 2.

1828 Sold as part of Hope Bowdler Estate to Moses G Benson. Described in sale details as 'Patch open to road'

1841 Census
Samuel Bowen - 56 Agric. Lab. d 5/2/49 aged 65
Mary ,, - 66 d 4/9/65 aged 93
Mary ,, - 34
John ,, - 8

1843 Valuation. Occupied by Samuel Bowen. 3r 0p
Estimated rental 15s 0d
Rateable value 12s 0d

1851 Census - uninhabited. It no longer appeared in any records.

Cwms Farm was part of the Bowdler Estate and when sold in 1828 was occupied by John Evans with 60 acres. By 1841 Thomas Jones was the tenant with 57 acres and 21 acres of Sheep Walk on Bowdler Hill and paid a rent of £34 11s 4d.

A description of the farm read "The House is built of stone and covered with brick tiles". It included a Brew house and three bedrooms "all in a very bad repair". The buildings built in stone and covered with Brosely tiles were, on the other hand, "in pretty good repair". The land was described as "very poor, cold and retentive soil, except a few arable fields next the hill. The grass and meadow land is very wet and wants draining. The landlord should be liberal in doing this draining, the tenant to carry the stones." It was said that the sun never shone on the farm for three months in the winter.

CWMS FARM - MAP No. 1.

1828 9 October - sold as part of the Hope Bowdler Estate Lot 11 "Dwelling House called The Cwms with 60 acres 2r 2p in the occupation of John Evans."

The property was owned by William Cheney Hart (dec'd) and bought by Moses George Benson.

1841 Census

Thomas Jones	- 60 Farmer
Margaret ,,	- 50
Sarah ,,	- 14
Edward ,,	- 11
Richard ,,	- 10
Ann ,,	- 7
Thomas Carter	- 21 Agric. Labourer

1843 Valuation. Occupied by Thomas Jones with 57 acres 2r 29p and 21 acres share of Sheep Walk.
Estimated Rental £34-11-4
Rateable Value £31-14-0

1851 Census

Ann Hills	- 64 Farmer (78 acres)
George ,,	- 32 Farmer's son
Sarah ,,	- 24
Lucy Penelope	- 1
Rheubin Davis	- 14 Agric. Labourer

1861 Census

John Carter	- 44 Farmer (60 acres)
Martha ,,	- 41
Jane ,,	- 10 m. ?/11/72 George George
William ,,	- 7
Ann ,,	- 5
Elizabeth ,,	- 2

1871 Census

John Carter	- 56 Farmer (66 acres) until 1879.
Martha ,,	- 52
William ,,	- 17
Ann ,,	- 15
Elizabeth ,,	- 12
John ,,	- 9
Ann ,,	- 6

1881 Census

John Rogers	- 38 Agric. Lab. m. 16/4/72 to Sarah E. Evans
Sarah ,,	- 28 d.2/6/1938 aged 85
Thomas ,,	- 7 Scholar
Esther ,,	- 7
Amy Harley	- 13 Servant

1885 J Roberts

1888 - 1900 John Miles

1905 - 1937 T Jarrett

1921	3 March	sold as part of Hope Bowdler Estate. Lot 12 "108 acres 3r 21p with living room, stone floor & grate. Sitting room with grate. Back kitchen boiler sink & tap. Cellar. 3 bedrooms. Partly walled garden. Tithe rent £9-1-0. Timber £44." Auction £1375 - withdrawn. Bought by Mr Jarrett. 1937 occupied by William Jarrett.

The Cwms Farm as it was in 1976, derelict.

The old Cwms farmhouse uninhabited and derelict.

Cwms Farm had various tenants until in 1921, when the Estate was broken up, it was sold to Wm. Jarrett with 108 acres. He lived there until a new farmhouse was built lower down in 1938 where he lived until around 1950. At that time he was wanting to build a bungalow near the old Toll House and when permission was not readily given, moved out of the farmhouse into an old double decker bus in the wood under the hill. The bungalow was eventually built and he went to live there when he gave up farming.

After the Toll House, there was no other house beside the road until arriving at the village of Hope Bowdler. However, on the right, a cart track ran from the gate at the junction with Bull Lane, up across the field to a small copse on the edge of Hazler Close to Hazler Barn. Attached to this was a cottage built of brick, stone and tiled roof, two rooms, pantry and back kitchen with bake oven and two bedrooms.

This was part of Lower House Farm. In the early 19th century some considered that with most farms being built in valley bottoms, there was a loss of benefit of the effluent from their middens and some farmers adopted a compromise solution, moving some of their flocks and herds to higher ground, building barns and a cottage, usually isolated and exposed, for a shepherd or herdsman. This may account for the location of this barn/cottage which was occupied without break until 1962. The Evans family lived there in 1870/80. The last occupant was Harold Musson, who had lived at Dryhill from 1946-59. He moved to Hope Bowdler after 1962 and today lives at Church Stretton. The building then became derelict and was demolished in 1980, some of the stone being used to build Tom Williamson's new house at Chelmick, where he works as a farrier.

As late as 1921 a stone quarry on the South East boundary of Hazler Barn was still being worked.

HAZLER BARN - MAP No. 4.

1828	sold as part of the Hope Bowdler Estate to Moses G Benson	
1841	Census	
	John Rogers	- 30 Agric. Lab. m. 31/1/31 to Ann Davies
	Ann ,,	- 30
	William ,,	- 10
1843	Valuation - probably included in Lower Farm details.	
1851	Census	
	Francis Harris	- 42 Agric. Lab.
	Mary ,,	- 40
	Mary ,,	- 21
	Samuel ,,	- 11
	Ann ,,	- 9
	Susanna ,,	- 8
	John ,,	- 4
	George ,,	- 2
1861	Census	
	Martin Carter	- 40 Labourer
	Elizabeth ,,	- 46
	Elizabeth ,,	- 10
	John ,,	- 7
	Richard ,,	- 7
	Joseph ,,	- 3
1871	Census	
	Thomas Eavans	- 47 Agric. Lab.
	Esther ,,	- 47
	Sarah ,,	- 19 m. 16/4/72 to John Rogers (Cwms)
	Thomas ,,	- 11
	John ,,	- 11 m. 8/7/84 to Sarah Davies

1881	Census	
	Thomas Eavans	- 56 Agric. Lab.
	Esther ,,	- 55 d. 6/1/89 aged 64
1921	Sold as part of Hope Bowdler Estate by R A Benson to George Preece. Sale details "brick", stone & tiled cottage. Living room with stove. Sitting room with grate & tiled floor. Pantry store cupboard. Back kitchen with boiler, sink & bake oven. Two bedrooms with grates." "Minerals-near S.E. boundary of the Hazler Barn is a large stone quarry approached by a good road. It is still being worked."	

Back on the Wenlock road, on the left-hand side as the road sweeps left, is the old Rectory.

In 1819, following the death of Mr. Cheney Hart, when the Hope Bowdler Estate was first put up for sale, it was "except for Parsonage House and Glebe lands of 25a 0r 1p". However, after the long delay while the sale was in the hands of Chancery courts in London between Margaret Pee and the Rev. George Watkin Marsh, the Estate sale was finally completed to the Benson family in 1828. At this subsequent sale the Rectory was Lot 1 and was then described as "Parsonage House, 45 acres of Glebe land and the tithes of the whole parish of about 1,670 acres".

The old Rectory, before being altered in 1862, note thatched roof.

At this time the Rectory was an attractive thatched house, L-shaped, of moderate size, and when Rev Marsh and his family lived there, they had just one female servant. Some parts of the house are very much older than the main construction and it is likely that a dwelling existed on the site as far back as the 13th or 14th Century, linked to the Church.

In 1862, Ralph Augustus Benson, Lord of the Manor and whose father Moses George was Patron of the Church, installed his son Riou George as Rector and, at the same time as the Church was being rebuilt, drastically altered and enlarged the Rectory by adding a second floor.

The old Rectory, after rebuilding.

Following the rebuilding, Rev Benson lived there throughout his incumbency until 1896 and raised a family of 13 children. At any one time there were employed in the house a governess, cook, nurse and nursemaid, kitchenmaid and housemaid.

RECTORY - HOPE BOWDLER - MAP No. 5.

1819/1828 Following the death of William Cheney Hart, the sale of the Rectory and the Hope Bowdler Estate was the subject of an action in the High Court in Chancery in London between Margaret Pee and George Watkin Marsh (the Rector). In 1828 at The Talbot Inn, Church Stretton on 9th October was sold by auction as Lot 1- "Parsonage House, 45 acres of Glebe land and the Tithes of the whole Parish of about 1670 acres."

1841 Census

Rev. George Marsh		- 65 Rector
Elizabeth	,,	- 30
Georgiana	,,	- 6
Isabella	,,	- 2
Elizabeth Garner		- 20 Female Servant

1851 Census
Uninhabited
12/3/52 John Croxton & John Rogers appointed to take Tithes etc. on the death of Rev. Marsh.

1856 Rev. G J Curtis. Elizabeth Curtis d. 15/11/54 aged 73

1861 Census
Uninhabited - period of rebuilding.

1863 Rev. Riou George Benson

1871 Census

Rev. Riou George Benson		- 36 Rector
Mary	,,	- 30
Edith Mary	,,	- 9
Riou Philip	,,	- 7
Edward Riou	,,	- 6
Madeleine Francis	,,	- 4
Dorothy Ann	,,	- 2
Philip Hinton	,,	- 10 mths d.4/11/85 at Shrewsbury School
Ann Selby		- 33 Cook
Elizabeth Jane Levington		- 30 Nurse
Mary Davis		- 24 Parlourmaid
Martha Pardoe		- 20 Under Nurse
Mary Jones		- 17 Kitchen Maid
William Harrington		- 20 Groom

1881 Census

Riou George Benson		- 46 Rector d. 21/1/96 aged 61
Madeleine	,,	- 14
Dorothy	,,	- 12
Aetheldreid	,,	- 9
Octavia	,,	- 7
Francis	,,	- 6
Charlotte	,,	- 4
Geoffrey	,,	- 3

John ,, - 10 mths. (Thomas 13th child)
Jane Reynolds - 34 Governess
Martha Chennington - 28 Cook
Francis Fasewell - 19 Nurse
Emily Watkins - 15 Nursemaid
Amy Rogers - 18 Kitchenmaid
Mary Croxton - 17 Housemaid

1921 Sold as part of Hope Bowdler Estate. Ceased to be a Rectory in 1950.

In 1902, at the time the Rev Jellicorse was Rector, Douglas and Clara Parr were tenants and for the next three years ran the Rectory as the 'Hope Bowdler Pension', taking in paying guests and providing a pony and trap service to Church Stretton railway station. In the winter of 1905 Clara fell while skating on Soudley Pools, fractured her skull and died. The family of four sons moved out of the area to Cardington and Plaish. The Rev and Mrs Mathews also took in guests during their years at the Rectory, making use of the large number of rooms it contained.

HOPE BOWDLER PENSION.

HOPE BOWDLER is a small village, 730 feet above sea level, situated amongst the beautiful hills of Church Stretton. It is a most delightful Summer and Winter Resort. The scenery around is not to be surpassed in the county. A walk of ten minutes from the house brings you to the top of the hill where one gets a grand panoramic view of Church Stretton, the surrounding hills and valley.

The House is large, comfortable, and splendidly situated in its own grounds, which contain Tennis and Croquet Lawns. The Golf Links are on the hills.

Accommodation for Motors and Cycles, Good Stabling, Horse and Trap, and Luggage Cart to meet trains.

Terms from 30/- weekly.

Meals—Breakfast 9 a.m. Luncheon 1 p.m.

Afternoon Tea 4.30. Dinner 7.

Sundays—Breakfast 9.30 a.m. Dinner 1 p.m.

Tea 5. Supper 9 p.m.

'lara Parr (née Bradley) aged 17*

Croquet on the Rectory lawn.

A new, modern Rectory was built in 1970 adjacent to Pykes Bank, and the old Rectory became a private house.

A little further up the road towards Much Wenlock, on the left, is a house known today as The Haven. In the 1819 sale catalogue it was listed as "Public House" fold and garden", and a few years later was referred to as "Hope Bowlder Inn". This is the only reference to any Inn or Ale house in the parish at any time. A comment around 1838 read "The custom at this house is but little, the farm is an indifferent state of culture, the arable land is much over-cropped". at this time 37a 1r 39p of land went with it, with an annual rental of £36 18s 0d.

'Hope Bowdler Inn', now 'The Haven' and, on the left, a modern conversion of the old adjoining buildings, now called 'Arcadia'.

There are records of its 3 bedrooms and 2 attic rooms being used to accommodate apprentices - 12 sleeping in one room!

By 1851 it no longer had any land attached and was occupied by a glazier, Jeremiah George. In 1854 the Hammond family moved in, and they were carpenters and wheelwrights, James Hammond being wheelwright to the Benson Estate. Their timber yard was where the stables and garage next to Thatches are today, and the Estate blacksmith shop was opposite the Croxton's house. Hammonds lived at the Haven until it was sold in 1921 when the house fetched £510, the building and yard adjoining another £115. This has since been converted into a dwelling.

The Haven was built in the mid-17the century, and is one of the few 'old' houses still occupied.

HOUSE & BUILDINGS - MAP No. 6.

1819 Part of Hope Bowdler Estate - no. 127 (old map) Public House, fold and Garden.

1828 Sold as Lot 6 "Dwelling house and buildings in the occupation of John Collins with several pieces of arable land and meadow land adjoining in the several occupations of John Collins, J Evans and T Lewis. 9 acres 1r 25p."

1838 Recorded as 'Hope Bowdler Inn, no 127 & lands. Small parlour, kitchen, dairy, brew house and cellar. 4 bedrooms. "The custom of this house is but little".'

1841 Census
John Collins - 60 Farmer d. 10/5/53 aged 71
Margaret ,, - 60 d. 1847
John Mason - 14 Agric. Lab.

1843 Valuation - 37a lr 39p and 18 acres share of sheep walk.
Estimated Rental £36-18-10. Rateable value £33-16-6.

1851 Census
Jeremiah George - 28 Glazier
Margaret ,, - 28
Sarah Margaret ,, - 7 mths

1861 Census
James Hammond - 40 Wheelwright m. 24/8/54 Mary Croxton
Mary ,, - 33
Sarah Madeleine - 6 m. 10/8/80 William Cox, Carpenter, Shrewsbury.
Jesse ,, - 1

1871 Census
James Hammond - 51 Carpenter d. 12/9/77 aged 57
Mary ,, - 44
Matilda ,, - 16
Jesse ,, - 11
William Cox - 17 Carpenter's apprentice m. 10/8/80 Sarah Hammond

1881 Census
Mary Hammond - 53 Laundress d. 24/12/1909 aged 82
Jesse ,, - 21 Carpenter
Philemon Jones - 18 Labourer
Henry Eavans - 16 Groom
Louisa Rogers - 14 Scholar
Emily Davies - 4

1921 Sold by R A Benson - Lot 7 "Opposite Manor Farm. Living room withm grate, tiled floor & boiler. Sitting room. Back kitchen with sink & pump, boiler and bake oven. 3 beds. 2 attic rooms'' Lot 8 was- ''buildings & yard adjoining let to Robert Jones, wheelwright.'' Well in Yard. Lot 7 & others had right to obtain water. Sold for £150, Lot 8 - £115.

Upper House Farm, note the daub and wattle at the rear.

A little further along is Upper House Farm. This is certainly one of the oldest properties in the village, part of it dating back to the 15th century with Norman arches in the cellars, although its outward appearance gives little indication of this, and the back wall is built of daub and wattle. '1485 built by Edwin Phipps' used to be visible on the chimney.

In 1841 it was some 115 acres with a rental of £133 2s. By 1871 this was increased to 160 acres, and ten years later was 185 acres. These increases were almost certainly due to amalgamating some of the small parcels of land that were earlier part of the small cottage holdings.

In 1838 it was described as 'a small farm house', yet it had 5 bedrooms and 3 attics. As was common practice at this time, it had some of its regular workers living in the house, as well as the family. The outbuildings were described as "being in bad repair" and the farm "generally in a very indifferent state of culture, badly managed and part of the farm in a very wet, unprofitable state for want of draining, but this tenant has not had the sense enough to perceive what would benefit him". This tenant was Thos. Lewis, soon to be followed by John Bluck who married a daughter of Rev. Marsh in 1825 and also farmed the Glebe lands.

Several well-known families farmed there from 1851, Richard Cartwright, John Pinches, Thomas Evans, and in 1897 George Preece, son of the nurseryman, was the tenant until 1921, when he bought it when the Estate was sold.

Upper House Farm

UPPER HOUSE FARM - MAP No. 7.

1828 Sold as part of Hope Bowdler Estate - Lot 3 "in the occupation of Thomas Lewis - 116 acres 2p" T Lewis married Jane Jones 7/10/1819

1841 Census

John Bluck - 41 Farmer m. Ann Shaw Marsh 30/5/25, d. 9/8/50 aged 51
Ann ,, - 40 d. 24/1/43 aged 42
Ann ,, - 15
Adah ,, - 13 m. 5/5/46 Thomas Gallears, farmer
George ,, - 11
William ,, - 9
Harriet ,, - 7
Maria ,, - 3
Henry Besnet - 21 Agric. Lab.
Charles Stubs - 20 Agric. Lab.
James Titley - 16 Agric. Lab.
William Harvey - 11 Agric. Lab.
Margaret Gough - 21 Female Servant

1843 Valuation - occupied by John Bluck 115 acres 33p and 67 acres share of sheep walk.
Estimated Rental £133-2-0
Rateable value £122-0-0

1851 Census

Richard Cartwright - 62 Farmer (115a)
Mary ,, - 54
Mary ,, - 28
Ellen ,, - 19 d. 23/5/51
Richard ,, - 21 d. 31/3/76 aged 46
Edwin ,, - 11
Ann Elsor - 12 Servant
Daniel Poston - 24 Servant

1861 Census

John Pinches - 46 Farmer (115a)
Sarah ,, - 50
Mary ,, - 20
Harriet ,, - 17
John ,, - 15
Jane ,, - 11
Richard Davis - 18
Benjamin Heighway- 15 Cowman

1871 Census

John Pinches - 55 Farmer (160a) d. 4/2/97 aged 86
Sarah ,, - 60 d. 25/3/80 aged 70
John ,, - 24 Farmer's son
Jane ,, - 20
H Corfield - 4 Grandson

	William Morny	- 25 General servant
	Edward Fox	- 18 General servant
1873	John Williams	- occupier
1881	Census	
	John Williams	- 48 Farmer (185a)
	Mary ,,	- 30
	Sarah ,,	- 10
	John ,,	- 8
	Ellen ,,	- 6
	Sarah ,,	- 5
	Edward ,,	- 4
	Mary ,,	- 2
	William Williams	- 24 Agric. Lab.
	Lucy ,,	- 22
	Mary ,,	- 1
	Thomas Williams	- 41 John's brother

1885-97 Thomas Evans occupier.

1897 George P Preece, occupier son of George Preece nurseryman & connected with building of Sandford Avenue.

1921 Sold as Lot 3. Auction price of £2000 withdrawn. Bought by George P Preece who lived there until 1936.

Continuing out of the village towards Wenlock, where the two modern houses and the Council houses stand today was all open fields. On the brow of the hill and off to the left stands Woodgate Cottage.

The acreage varied over the years. In 1828 it was sold as 'The Woodgate' with 78a 1r 4p, and in 1841 it was 65a 3r 34p with a share of 110 acres of Sheep walk and a rental of £77 7s 10d. It appears, during this period, to have been farmed in with Manor Farm.

In 1838 the description read "the House is built with stone walls and thatch cover and consists of small parlour, kitchen, dairy and pantry in pretty good order". That description, apart from it now having a tiled roof and being in a poor state of repair, fits the sale details when sold in 1985. The farm - 1838 - was "in bad condition, is very poor, very few turnips and no clover". The house and building appear to have remained unchanged for at least 150 years, and it is probably considerably older. In 1821 it was sold for £610.

Woodgate Cottage, sometimes called 'The Woodgate'. Now demolished and a modern house and holiday flats built on the site.

WOODGATE COTTAGE Tithe No. 65 - MAP No. 13.

1828 Sold as part of Hope Bowdler Estate Lot 8 "Farm house & buildings called 'The Woodgate' in the occupation of John Pritchart & Mr Adams 78a 1r 4p property of late W C Hart & bought by Moses George Benson.

1841 Census - unoccupied.

1843 Valuation - 65a 3r 34p & 110 acres share of Sheep Walk. Estimated rental £77-7-10. Rateable value £70-18-0

1851 Census - unoccupied.

1861 Census
John Humphries - 39 Labourer
Ellen ,, - 31 Emma Humphries - 7
John ,, - 4 George ,, - 3

1871 Census
George Eavans - 29 Agric. Lab.
Susan ,, - 27
Priscilla ,, - 5

1881 Census - unoccupied

1921 Sold by R A Benson. 45 acres Timber value £29 Lot 5 for £610.

1937 Bought by William Thomas Willis, whose family farmed there until 1984.

Woodgate Farm, Wall Bank. Originally an agricultural labourer's cottage.

Adjoining this property was Woodgate Farm. In 1828 the Sale details listed this as Lot 10 with 41a 0r 19p. There was no Farm house at that time. By 1843 it was reduced to 21a 3r 12p and a rental of £18 11s 11d. There were, however, two small cottages occupied by agricultural workers, with an annual rent of £3 and situated in field no. 55 - Cabbage Field - listed in the 1841 census. By 1851 one of these was 'uninhabited' and is probably the site of a small modern house today, whereas the other cottage almost certainly became the 'farm house' as we know it today, and was occupied by Francis George who, as well as farming the land, worked as a stonemason, as did his son Edward. He died in 1877, when John Grainger moved in and continued in occupation until 1926, having bought it in 1921. His son William was still farming there in 1937.

WOODGATE FARM Tithe No. 55 - MAP No. 14.

1928 Sold as part of Hope Bowdler Estate Lot 10 - 41a 19p.

1841 Census - no house went with the land -

1843 Valuation - occupied by John Sankey 21a 3r 12p
Estimated rental £18-11-11 Rateable value £17-0-0

1851 Census
Francis George - 24 Farmer (24a)
Charlotte ,, - 25
George ,, - 4 mths

1861 Census
Francis George - 38 Stonemason
Charlotte ,, - 38
George - 11 m.?/11/72
Jane Carter
Jeremiah ,, - 8 d.13/12/80 aged 28
Edwin ,, - 5 d.28/3/77
Mary Ann ,, - 3
Thomas ,, - 4 mths

1871 Census
Francis George - 46 Farmer (22a) d.7/12/77
Charlotte ,, - 46 d.13/1/74 aged 49
Edward ,, - 15 Mason
Mary ,, - 12 Thomas George George - 9
Elizabeth ,, - 6 William George George - 7 mths

1881 Census
James Grainger - 40 Farmer (25a)
Sarah ,, - 40 d.27/7/1904 aged 64
Mary ,, - 10 Scholar
William ,, - 7 m.21/6/1901 Elizabeth Pugh
d.15/12/1949 aged 75
Gertrude ,, - 4
Sarah ,, - 2 d.5/3/95 aged 16

1921 Sold as Lot 4 by R A Benson. Timber value £9.

WALL BANK - MAP No. 16.

1841 Census
Mathew Hall - 30 Agric. Lab. m. 27/9/32 Martha Mawn
Martha ,, - 30
John ,, - 10 Henry Hall - 6
Benjamin ,, - 4 Mathew ,, - 1

1843 Valuation - Estimated rental £3-0-0 Rateable value £2-10-0

No further reference to this cottage but, in 1851 was probably the house for Woodgate Farm.

WALL BANK - MAP No. 15.

1841 Census

Thomas Mawn	- 50 Agric. Lab.	
Margaret ,,	- 55 Samuel Mawn	- 20
Zillah ,,	- 15 James Mathews	- 8

1843 Valuation - Estimated rental £3-0-0 Rateable value £2-10-0

No further reference to this cottage. A modern house was built on the site by Sarah Grainger.

Woodgate Farm forms the Eastern edge of the Parish. Returning back down the road towards the village there are no houses on the left until the barns of Manor Farm, behind which is the Hall. This has, at various times, been referred to as Hope Bowdler Hall, Hope Bowdler Manor, the Manor House and Manor Farm.

Hope Bowdler Hall

In the writer's opinion there is no doubt that this was a 17th century or early 18th century house, which at some time was enlarged. It had considerable gardens, stables and some barns, etc., but it was never the Manor House. In the 1700's the Lutwyche family owned several manors in the area and these amounted to several thousand acres in total. Following the death of William Lutwyche in 1785 much of this land was sold, and among the Lots in Hope Bowdler was Lot XIX, "Manor of Hope Bowdler". This almost certainly only referred to the title and lands of the 'manor' which amounted to some 222 acres in two farms let to Francis Hall and Edward Thomas, (corresponding roughly to Upper and Lower farms today) and the right to various small rents from other properties. There is no mention of 'The Hall' in this sale, and it may be that Mr. Cheney Hart had already purchased it, together with other land and properties to form the Hope Bowdler Estate which, after his death, was sold en bloc to Moses George Benson.

During the 1800's, with all the land in the Estate being under one ownership, most of the fields that went with the cottages, the two main farms and the lands with the Hall were rearranged so that the Hall had a farm of some 200 acres by 1861, later reduced to 175 when it was sold in 1921 as Manor Farm.

In the Sale catalogue of 1819 it was referred to as 'Hope Bowdler Hall' and, in the text, "the mansion house, offices and garden, fit for the accommodation of a gentleman's family". At this time all the other tenants were served notice to quit one year later. For legal reasons the sale of the Estate was held up until 1828 when Moses George Benson was the purchaser, but he never lived in the house. His agent, William Adams, was already living there with his wife, Ann Wilding.

In 1838 Hope Bowdler Mansion as it was then described was "built with stone and part with brick and consists of Hall entrance and two Parlours on the S W front, Dining Room and Drawing Room over on the S E front, Study, Servants Hall, Kitchen, Brewhouse, Dairy, Larder, Press room, Tub room, Cheese room, Store room, a Bath walled round with roof over, a small beer cellar, an Ale cellar, a large vault built for ale, wine etc. under the lawn, Five best bedrooms and four attick rooms". The Buildings included stables for horses, cowhouse and piggery. A four-stalled Hack Stable was "very damp and unfit for horses in consequence of a spring being underneath the foundation."

"The house and buildings are (generally speaking) *in bad repair"*. Part of the house was occupied by Robert Hart and the remainder by William Adams. The lands were "by no means in a good state of cultivation" whereas the Farm "could be much improved by more judicious attention to the irrigation and a more regular course of Turnip husbandry".

MANOR FARM/THE HALL - MAP No. 12.

1819 October 21 - sale of the Manor of Hope Bowdler, the property of the late William Cheney Hart, with its Appurtenances and the Advowson or the perpetual right of presentation to the Rectory of Hope Bowdler subject to the incumbency of George W Marsh, now aged 46, together with the Mansion House, offices, garden and appurtenances called 'Hope Bowdler Hall' (described as fit for the accommodation of a gentleman's family). Other occupants/tenants served notice to quit 25/3/1820 Samuel Medlicott, John Evans, Bezaleel Croxton, George Corfield, John Collins, William George, Edward Jones, Amos Mawn, John Ellis, John Sankey, John Griffiths, Thomas Wenlock. 1155 acres 2r 19p.

except for Parsonage House, Glebe lands 25a 0r 1p, Small piece of land 3r 34p belonging to Corporation of Shrewsbury. 2 small houses belonging to widow Gough and Blacksmith's house & garden 1r 2p belonging to Bezaleel Croxton.

There then followed a 9 year action in the High Court, Chancery, London between Margaret Pee & George Watkin Marsh until ...

1828 October 9th By Auction at the Talbot Inn, Church Stretton Lot 12 "Manor of Hope Bowdler - 75 acres - in occupation of Mr Adams also 2 cottages and an orchard in occupation of Amos Mawn & Rowland Galliers" Bought by Moses George Benson.

1841 Census

William Adams	- 45 Farmer m. 3/7/28 Ann Wilding
John ,,	- 45 brother
Ann ,,	- 35 d. 29/3/51 aged 56
Ann Wilding	- 13
Sarah Yapp	- 20 Female servant
Mary Barron	- 15 ,, ,,
William Edwards	- 25 Agric. Lab.
Edward Rea	- 25 ,, ,,
Samuel Dodd	- 20 ,, ,,
Samuel Russell	- 15 ,, ,,
William Davies	- 15 ,, ,,

1843 Valuation - 148a 2r 34p Estimated rental £137-2-2
Rateable value £125-13-6

1851 Census

William Adams	- 57 Farmer d. 29/3/56 aged 63
John ,,	- 54 brother
Ann Wilding	- 20 niece Housekeeper
James Cleaton	- 28 Agric. Lab.
Richard Coins	- 37 ,, ,,
Edward Blakeway	- 18 ,, ,,

	John Jones	- 14 ,, ,,
	Mary Powell	- 14 Housemaid
	Emma Lane	- 15 ,,
	John Corfield	- 20 Visitor
	Mary Hoop	- 62 ,,
1861	Census	
	Richard Wellings	- 47 Farmer (200a)
	Sarah ,,	- 41
	Sarah ,,	- 18 Richard Wellings - 11
	Mary ,,	- 16 John ,, - 5
	Ann ,,	- 13 Charlotte ,, - 2
	Charles Miles	- 25 Shepherd
	Samuel Wilkes	- 23 Carter
	Charles Painter	- 18 Cowman

1871 Census - no Farmer was referred to but against 'Farm House' was listed:-

William Burgess	- 25 Agric. Lab.
Jane ,,	- 21
Martha Lewis	- 12

Three of the old barns, Manor Farm, have been converted into houses.

1877 either George Charlton or John Hodge in occupation

1881 Census - no reference

1885-91 George Robinson in occupation

1895-1921 Thomas Hartley Sen & Jun in occupation

1921 Sold as part of Hope Bowdler Estate. Auction - £3150 withdrawn. Bought by George P Preece. 1941-74 lived in by George E Preece. 1974-77 by G F W Preece, who still farms the land. 1977 bought by Col. J. Inglis.

Continuing a few yards further along the road was a small cottage with garden and orchard "built with Timber Lath and Plaster walls with tile cover". In 1838 it was occupied by a Mr. Rogers with an annual rental of £4. It was lived in until the late 1800's when it was demolished. When the Estate was sold in 1921 as Lot 10 it fetched £35. Today, a modern house 'Burnbrae' stands on the old cottage site.

HOUSE & GARDEN Tithe No. 85 MAP No. 11.

1828 Sold as part of Hope Bowdler Estate

1841 Census
William Williams - 35 Agric. Lab. m. 23/6/34
E. Griffiths
Elizabeth ,, - 28
Edwin ,, - 7 Emma Williams - 3
William ,, - 5 Infant - 1 mth

1843 Valuation - Estimated rental £4-0-0 1r 12p
Rateable value £3-4-0

1851 Census
William Williams - 44 Agric. Lab.
Eliza ,, - 38 wife & Farmer's boy
William ,, - 14
Emma ,, - 12 Hannah Williams - 5
Thomas ,, - 10 Zellah ,, - 3
Susanna ,, - 7 George ,, - 9 mths

1861 Census
William Williams - 52 Labourer d. 3/9/68
Edwin ,, - 26 ,,
Susannah ,, - 17
Hannah ,, - 15 John Griffith - 8
Zellah ,, - 13 Henry ,, - 5
George ,, - 10 Charles ,, - 3

1871 Census
Mary Jones - 41 widow-dressmaker
Elizabeth - 9
Eliza ,, - 3

1881 Census
John Price - 54 Farm Labourer m. 27/5/72
d. 15/3/1912
Mary ,, - 51
Eliza ,, - 13 Scholar

The old Smithy and Carpenter's Shop on the left of 'The Waste', with the Church Walk on the right.

At the bottom of the hill, in the centre of the village, was an open space on the N E side of the Church. This was referred to in 1838 as "The waste" and may have been the "small piece of land 3r 34p belonging to the Corporation of Shrewsbury", and this was not part of the Hope Bowdler Estate when put up for sale in 1819. The area still exists today with a right of way to The Hall and other houses and a Public footpath running along the side nearest the Church.

Near the road, on the corner, is the old Smithy built by Bezaleel Croxton in 1797. Next to this is a Carpenter's shop built in 1821 by Rowland Gallears.

The old Smithy

A little further along, on the left, is the Blacksmith's House which is certainly one of the oldest in the village, and was probably lived in by John and Joan Croxton when they married in 1715. At that time it was owned by the Lord of the Manor, William Lutwyche, but in 1759 he gave the house to John Croxton together with Five Guineas in exchange for two fields known as Two Butts and Three Butts. It was never part of the Hope Bowdler Estate.

At least one of the Croxton family was a blacksmith throughout some 200 years. They were also very involved in the Parish as Clerks to the Parish (John, born 1805, was Clerk for 65 years), Constables, Churchwardens and Road overseers. They also rented land for farming and used to run a haulage business.

There was also a weaving shop in the house which Shimrah Croxton operated from 1770 to 1800.

Adjoining the Blacksmith's house was a small thatched cottage (originally outbuildings) in which he used to house people on an annual rental basis, with an additional charge for use of the garden.

The house still stands today, very much in its original state.

BLACKSMITH'S HOUSE - MAP No. 9.

1759 The house was given to John Croxton by William Lutwyche together with £5-5-0 in exchange for two fields known as Two Butts and Three Butts. It was never part of the W C Hart or Benson Hope Bowdler Estate.

1841 Census

John Croxton	- 45	Smithy m.25/8/1823 Catherine Collins Shuker
Catherine ,,	- 35	
Francis ,,	- 15	
John ,,	- 15	
Sarah ,,	- 12	
Betsy ,,	- 10	
Bezaleel ,,	- 8	

	Ann ,,	- 6
	Philip ,,	- 4
	Katherine ,,	- 10 mths
1851	Census	
	John Croxton	- 54 Blacksmith
	Catherine ,	- 49 d. 17/10/53 aged 52
	John ,,	- 26 Blacksmith m. Oct/54 Jane Catherall
	Betsy ,,	- 19 m. 15/2/58 Joseph Werks, Labourer, Ragdon
	Bezaleel ,,	- 17 Blacksmith
	Ann ,,	- 14
	Philip ,,	- 12 Scholar
	Katherine ,,	- 10
	Emma ,,	- 6
	George ,,	- 4
	John Collins	- 71 Agric. Lab. Father-in-Law
	Robert Morgan	- 14 ,, ,,
1861	Census	
	John Croxton	- 68 Farmer
	Bezaleel ,,	- 26 Blacksmith
	Ann Maria,,	- 24
	Philip ,,	- 22 Wheelwright m. 9/2/64 Ann Mason
	Katherine ,,	- 20
	George ,,	- 16
	John Dodd	- 20 Carter
	Richard Ward	- 14 Ploughboy
1871	Census	
	John Croxton	- 75 Blacksmith d. 8/5/76 aged 79
	Bezaleel ,,	- 37 " assistant
	Eliza ,,	- 36 Wife
	Mary ,,	- 7 m. 23/4/94 John George, Carpenter, Shrewsbury
	Lewis ,,	- 3
	John Jeremiah	- 1
1881	Census	
	Bezaleel Croxton	- 47 Blacksmith d. 29/12/1902 aged 68
	Eliza ,,	- 46 d. 22/9/1822
	Louis ,,	- 13
	John ,,	- 11
	Bezaleel ,,	- 9 d. 30/7/1904 aged 32
	Thomas ,,	- 7 m. 11/4/1909 Marion Thomas d. 8/2/1941 aged 67
	Sarah ,,	- 5 m. 30/4/1913 Arthur Lewis

A little further on, across the road leading to the Hall, is another of the very old houses - Thatches. This was at times occupied by two families, Amos Mawn and Rowland Gallears in 1819, and at other

'Thatches', originally semi-detached. The home of wheelwrights for over 100 years.

times by just one family. It had a rental value of £5 16s 0d a year, and was occupied by either the Gallears or Jones family - both wheelwrights - from this time until its sale in 1921 for £165, with the carpenter's shop fetching £35. There was a saw-pit in the 'waste' nearly opposite the carpenter's shop.

It seems likely that there was some friction between Croxton and Gallear, as a reference in 1838 states "he (Gallear) is in dispute with the blacksmith respecting a patch of land behind his shop, and he should be supported in this, otherwise the blacksmith will claim the land as his own."

HOUSE & GARDEN Tithe No. 99 - MAP No. 10.

1828 Included with the sale of the Manor House, then semi-detached, in occupation Amos Mawn and Rowland Gallears.

1841 Census
Richard Gallears - 46 Wheelwright
Ann ,, - 42 John Gallears - 6

	John ,,	- 21			
	Betsey ,,	- 20	Ann ,,	- 10	
	Jane ,,	- 8	Edwin ,,	- 6	
	Henry ,,	- 4	Hillary ,,	- 3 mths	

1843 Valuation - House, garden & wheelwrights Shop - 2r 7p Estimated rental £7-0-0
Rateable value £5-16-0

1851 Census

John Jones	- 39	Wheelwright m. 14/12/43 Emma Griffiths
Emma ,,	- 41	d. 13/11/53 aged 44
Humphrey ,,	- 6	Fanny Jones - 2
Herbert ,,	- 4	John ,, - 2 mths
Eliza Sebrey	- 18	Housemaid
Richard Cambrill	- 15	Apprentice

1861 Census

John Jones	- 48	Wheelwright m. 24/9/56 Maria Hughes
Maria ,,	- 31	Wife (2nd)
Alfred ,,	- 16	
Fanny ,,	- 12	Mary Hughes - 7
John ,,	- 10	George ,, - 2
Robert ,,	- 2	Eliza ,, - 21 visitor
Mary Hughes	- 7	
George ,,	- 2	

1871 Census

John Jones	- 60	Wheelwright/carpenter
Maria ,,	- 40	
Herbert ,,	- 25	Wheelwright/carpenter
Robert ,,	- 12	Arthur Jones - 4
Henry ,,	- 8	Elizabeth ,, - 1
Ellen ,,	- 5	Emily ,, d. 14/8/72 aged 6 mths

1881 Census

John Jones	- 73	Wheelwright d. 19/5/84 aged 75
Maria ,,	- 49	d. 7/9/1911
Robert ,,	- 22	Wheelwright d. 7/5/1947
Henry ,,	- 18	Grocer
Arthur ,,	- 14	Scholar
Elizabeth ,,	- 11	d. 26/12/88 aged 19
Minnie ,,	- 4	
Lily ,,	- 2	

1921 Sold - "Lot 6 Water from Manor House Dairy by gravitation from a well in field 103 in Upper Farm. Living & sitting rooms with cupboards. Back kitchen with boiler & bake oven, larder, 2 bedrooms." Also Lot 8 - buildings & yard and Lot 10 - Garden (site of Burnbrae) adjoins Manor Farm and Road frontage. Lot 6 - £165. Lot 8 (adjoins No. 7 H.B.) - £115. Lot 10 - £35. Lot 9 - Stone & tiled wheelwright's shop -£35

Coming back along 'The Waste' with the Church lying on your left there is, on the corner, Lower House Farm as it is known today. In 1828 it was known as "Evans Farm", but much earlier in an Indenture dated 2nd September 1692 between Edward Lutwyche and Benjamin Philips for a rent of £18 6s 0d it refers to "Church Stile House Farm". It is probable that this is the same place.

The farm, in 1843, was 213 acres with a rental of £210 18s 0d. In three of the census returns 1851, '71 and '81 no entry for those living there can be directly connected to the farm. However, there were three families of farm labourers recorded in 1871 and '81 for whom no house can be traced, so it is probable that when the Haynes family of Ragdon were farming the land, they were installed in the farmhouse.

In 1838 the description read "The Farm House is a very inferior one built part with stone walls, part with timber walls with lath and plaster, the roof covered with brick tiles and comprises a small Parlour

Lower House Farm, sometime known as 'Evan's Farm and 'Church House Stile Farm'.

with stone floor, Kitchen, Brewhouse, Dairy and Cellar, with 4 bedrooms''. (In 1921 the sale details include 'secondary staircase leading to a Men's room'). It goes on to say ''This tenant (Mr. Oakley) seems to be an improving, painstaking person - his predecessor (Mr. Evans) I think must have left the Farm in a bad state of cultivation ... a great portion of the land is in such a foul state that it cannot all be followed for turnips which require it. Some of these lands, I have been informed, have grown 4, 5, 6 and 7 crops in succession, enough to ruin any land''.

LOWER HOUSE FARM - MAP No. 8.

1692 An indenture dated 2/9/1692 between Edward Lutwyche and Benjamin Phillips of a farm called 'Church Stile House Farm' for a rent of £18-6-0 was almost certainly this farm.

1828 Sold as Lot 2 ''Evans Farm, in the occupation of John Evans 198 acres 39p.''

1841 Census

Thomas Oakley - 70 Farmer
Thomas ,, - 15
Joseph Hollybrook - 45 Male Servant
Harriet ,, - 45 Female Servant
John Jones - 25 Agric. Lab.
John Raisin - 12 Agric. Lab.
Richard Bason - 13 Agric. Lab.
Ann Poston - 20 Female Servant
Mary Croxton - 14 ,, ,,

1843 Valuation - occupied by Thomas Oakley with 213 acres and 110 acres of sheep walk.
Estimated Rental £216-18-0
Rateable value £198-16-6

1851 Census - uninhabited

1861 Census

Francis Bishop - 66 Farmer (200a) d. 2/1/72
Francis ,, - 38 son d. 16/3/89 in Union Workhouse
Ann ,, - 33 d. 6/3/74 suddenly from heart disease
Lizzie ,, - 24
Sarah ,, - 22
Edwin ,, - 17
Thomas Adams - 28 Carter d. 3/4/87 aged 55
John Pinches - 21 Shepherd

1871 Census

Richard Poston - 53 Agric. Lab.
Sarah ,, - 35 sister

	Philip ,,	- 37 Agric. Lab. d. 26/11/79 aged 46
	Sarah ,,	- 31
	William ,,	- 6 Margaret Poston - 4
	John ,,	- 2
1881	Census	
	Charles Merrick	- 24 Farm Labourer
	Mary ,,	
	Louisa ,,	- 5 mths
	Evan Jones	- 28 Farm Labourer
	Elizabeth ,,	- 30
	Caroline ,,	- 3
	Sarah ,,	- 1

1921 Sold as Lot 2 "Hope Bowdler Farm 176 acres. House details include secondary staircase leading to a mens room. 4 bedrooms & box room."
Tithe Rent £30-15-0. Timber value £66.
Auction - £3350 - withdrawn. Bought by G P Preece, lived in and farmed by W & F Preece until 1972 when sold to G James with 216 acres, hill cow and sheep subsidy worth £1500 in 1972. Long Mynd grazing rights for 300 sheep and 50 ponies.

An 18th Century cottage demolished in 1970 when the Morris family sold it. 'Gaerstone Lodge' has been built on the site.

Leaving the village along the road towards Ticklerton, next door to Lower House Farm, was The School for 48 children, built in 1856. This was closed in 1948 and is now a private house. Map No. 8A.

About a mile further along this road are three cottages on the right hand side. All built around 1730. The first one was occupied by James Sheffield, certainly from 1794, and had a rental of £2 10s 0d plus 6s 0d for the garden. He was a Mason and it is likely that the road up to Chelmick Valley called Sheffield Lane was named after him. After the war Richard Morris lived there, with a barn and fields opposite, until he sold it and the house became derelict. In 1970 a new house, Gaerstone Lodge, was built on the site.

SOUDLEY - GARDEN & HOUSE Tithe No. 114 - MAP No. 17.

1841	Census	
	James Sheffield	- 50 Mason m. 11/6/27 Mary Hammond
	Mary ,,	- 40 d. 14/5/49
	Thomas ,,	- 10
	Sarah ,,	- 5 d. 15/1/59 aged 22
1843	Valuation - Estimated rental - House £2-10-0, garden 6-0	
	Rateable value - House £2-2-0, garden 5-6	
1851	Census	
	Elizabeth Howell	- 53 Pauper & Charwoman
	Mary ,,	- 39
	Sarah ,,	- 10 Thomas Howell - 8
1861	Census	
	Elizabeth Hince	- 60 Widow, shopkeeper d. 17/2/64 aged 65
	Sarah ,,	- 18 m. 25/2/62 Samuel Jarrett
1871	Census	
	Thomas Hince	- 41 Agric. Lab.
1881	Census	
	Thomas Hince	- 50 unmarried Farm Labourer d. 17/3/97

Next door, with a rent of £3 10s 0d for house and garden, was Lilac Cottage which still stands today, very much in its original state. Here John Griffith operated as a Grocer in 1824. One can only assume that he carried on his business by travelling around the area to sell his goods, as there were no facilities nor sufficient local people to give him a living. Later he was listed as a butcher until his death at 69 in 1852. The use of the word 'butcher' here (and elsewhere) meant that

'Lilac Cottage', built in 1730.

he was someone who did the butchering of pigs, etc. for those people who kept and fattened animals for their own use. The glazier, Jeremiah George, who married Francis Croxton, then moved here from the Haven. This cottage is probably one of the best, and least altered, examples of an 18th century stone cottage in the area.

SOUDLEY- HOUSE & GARDEN Tithe No. 113 - MAP No. 18.

1841 Census
John Griffith - 59 Butcher
Hannah ,, - 57 Emma Griffith - 30
Fanny ,, - 14 Emma Bowdler - 5

1843 Valuation - Estimated Rental £3-10-0 Rateable value £2-18-0

1851 Census
John Griffith - 68 Butcher d. 1/12/52 aged 69
Fanny ,, - 22
Emma Bowdler - 12 Gd-daughter

1861 Census
Jeremiah George - 35 Glazier m. 12/2/50 Francis Croxton
Francis ,, - 35
Sarah ,, - 10
Mary Ann ,, - 9
William Henry,, - 5

1871 Census
Francis Bishop - 75 (late farmer Lower Farm) d. 21/1/72
Ann ,, - 40 d. 6/3/74 (heart disease)
Sarah ,, - 32

1881 Census
Benjamin Colley - 44 Farm Labourer d. 3/5/1900 aged 65
Ann ,, - 40
Ellen ,, - 14 William Colley - 12 Scholar d. 19/3/82
Edwin ,, - 7 Eliza ,, - 10 ,,
John ,, - 6 Harriet ,, - 4
Matilda ,, - 3 Jesse ,, - 1

The third house in the row which was thatched, was of similar size and bordered on the edge of the Parish boundary. It too had a rental of £3 10s 0d, and for some fifty years James Carter lived there, first as a butcher and then as agricultural labourer. Later, a fearsome looking man, George Williams with a very large beard and a wooden leg lived there. He died aged 77 (13/2/1919). School children used to scuttle by on the other side of the road when he was leaning over his gate. The house was burnt down in 1930 and was never rebuilt, and is now part of Lilac Cottage garden.

SOUDLEY - HOUSE & GARDEN Tithe No. 112 - MAP No. 19.

1841 Census
Samuel Williams - 40 Agric. Lab.
Mary ,, - 40
Thomas ,, - 9 Agric. Lab.
Samuel ,, - 6 Elizabeth Williams - 8
John ,, - 2

1843 Valuation - Est Rental £3-10-0 Rateable value £2-18-0

1851 Census
Samuel Williams - 51 Road labourer
Mary ,, - 54
Thomas ,, - 19

1861 Census
James Carter - 36 Butcher
Eliza ,, - 34
Alfred ,, - 8 Mary Carter - 6
Charles ,, - 4 Emma ,, - 2

1871	Census	
	James Carter	- 41 Agric. Lab.
	Eliza ,,	- 41 Charles Carter - 13
	Emma ,,	- 10 George ,, - 8
	Maria ,,	- 7 Ann ,, - 2
1881	Census	
	James Carter	- 50 Agric. Lab. d. 3/1/1903
	Eliza ,,	- 50 d. 29/9/95
	Ann ,,	- 12
	William ,,	- 9
	House burnt down and never rebuilt.	

'Carter's Cottage', burnt down and never rebuilt. Now forms part of the garden of 'Lilac Cottage'.

George Williams.

There is just one other house shown to be 'uninhabited' in the 1841 census, and as lived in by George Poston and John Sebrey in the 1851 census. No other mention is made of this dwelling, but it could be the 'house in ruins' shown on the 1819 Sale map and located just before the dip and about 300 yards from the School, on the same side of the road. Map No. 19B.

1841 Census - uninhabited. Possibly house shown in 1819 Sale details of W C Hart as "53 - House in ruins"

1843 Valuation - not listed

1851 Census

George Poston	- 23	Agric. Lab.
Margaret ,,	- 29	Wife
Robert ,,	- 6	
Emma ,,	- 2	
Edwin ,,	- 8 mths	
John Sebrey	- 21	Agric Lab m.23/4/49 Ann Cadwallader
Ann ,,	- 23	wife
Alfred ,,	- 8 mths	

No further mention is made of this dwelling - in the 1851 Census was listed as 'No. 1 Soudley'.

Although no reference is made to it on either the Tithe map or the 1819 Sale map, there was probably a house high on Bowdler Hill, as the remains of an old garden and signs of an enclosed area are still to be seen in the field number 38, known as 'Old House Leasow'.

Within the Parish of Hope Bowdler are two townships - Ragdon and Chelmick.

RAGDON - PEOPLE AND HOUSES

There were three ways of getting there. At the Toll House at Hazler Gate, by turning right up a narrow track known as Ghost Hole Lane, across Hazler Hill and along below the Ragleth Hill. Or by taking the cart track - Bull Lane - to the right just before the Wenlock Road enters Hope Bowdler, and joining the road from Chelmick to follow the same road below the Ragleth. The third way was from Acton Scott with six gates along the road. Whichever way you approached, Ragdon was just two farms, the first one you come to being Upper or Ragdon Manor Farm.

Ragdon Manor Farm.

In the garden is a sundial dated 1707 and this may well be around the time when this particular house was built, almost certainly on the site of an earlier building. The house today is rendered over stone blocks, and the stone construction is typical of the post-Elizabethan era when agriculture (sheep and wool) was on the upturn. The principal, workers lived in, having their own staircase and rooms, separate from the family.

In 1800 the farm was owned by Charles Price Stanier, later handed down to his son. The last reference to them was in 1889 when they had left the country and were mining in the North Western Territory of Canada. In 1809 the rent was £132 10s 0d, by 1839 it had risen to £200, and a valuation in 1843 put it at £175 5s 8d for 178 acres.

The Haynes family lived there and farmed it from 1800 (or earlier) to 1894. They were in a big way of farming because, at times, they also rented and farmed Chelmick Manor Farm and Lower House Farm in Hope Bowdler, making 450 acres in total.

In 1894 the farm was let to Richard Wilding for four years at £170 a year. Then, in 1911, two parcels of land were sold - Upper and Lower Moors and Ragbatch, reducing the farm to 154 acres.

In 1920 the Stanier family sold it for £3,200 and four years later it went for £2,800. Finally, in 1947, Alfred Perkins bought it for £4,000, soon adding the Upper and Lower Dol ground - formerly Glebe land - for £400.

RAGDON MANOR FARM - MAP No. 20.

1804 Robert Haynes married Martha Beddows 21st May

1809 Yearly rent £132-10-0 - owned by Charles Price Stanier

1831 Robert Haynes died 10 June

1839 Yearly rent £200-0-0 - owned by John Stanier

1841 Census

Martha Haynes	- 60 Farmer
Mary ,,	- 28
Robert ,,	- 25 Farmer
Susan Haynes	- 17
Ann ,,	- 15 m. 3/6/50 William Spence
Philemon ,,	- 15
Adah Whitmore	- 6 m. 12/5/58 George Goring, grocer from Worcester
John Lowe	- 25 Agric Lab
William Moile	- 18 ,, ,,
Thomas Raisin	- 20 ,, ,,
Jeremiah George	- 15 ,, ,,
Benjamin ,,	- 10 ,, ,,
John Morris	- 14 ,, ,,
Eliza Haines	- 17 Female servant

1843 Valuation - 178 acres 1r 9p Estimated rental £175-5-8 Rateable value £160-13-0

1851 Census

Martha Haynes	- 72 Farmer (182a)
Susan ,,	- 28 Farmer's daughter
Philemon ,,	- 24 Farmer's son
Mary ,,	- 22 wife

William Jones - 25 Agric Lab
? ? - 13 ,, ,,
Edward ? - 38 ,, ,,
Mary ? - 35 wife
Eleanor ?

1861 Census
Philemon Haynes - 37 (200a)
Mary ,, - 32 William Haynes - 10
Robert ,, - 8 Jane ,, - 6
Philemon ,, - 4 James ,, - 8 mths
Martha ,, - 81 Mother d. 25/6/70 aged 90
Sarah ? - 19 Housemaid
Elizabeth Wainwright - 16 Dairymaid
Thomas Cole - 21 Shepherd
Thomas Owen - 19 Waggoner
Samuel Gwilliam - 17 Cowman
Henry Mason - 11 Plougboy

1867 John Stanier died

1871 Census
Philemon Haynes - 46 Farmer (450a)
Mary ,, - 40
William ,, - 19 d. 6/3/1919 aged 68
Robert ,, - 17 d. 31/5/1920 aged 66 suddenly on the Shrewsbury Road on way to the Infirmary
Jane ,, - 16 m. 22/10/79 Thomas Jones
Philemon ,, - 14
James ,, - 10
Mary ,, - 9
Harry ,, - 7
John ,, - 5
Edward ,, - 3
Emma Griffiths - 18 General servant
William Perkins - 19 Waggoner
James Powell - 19 Cowman
Edwin Harley - 17 Waggoner
Edwin Eavans - 16 Groom
William Mason - 25 General servant
James Gardner - 44 Occasional servant

1881 Census
Philemon Haynes - 57 Farmer (470a) d. 2/3/1900 aged 77
Mary ,, - 51 d. 16/5/1900 aged 71
Robert ,, - 27
James ,, - 20
Mary ,, - 19 Scholar
Charles ,, - 16
Edward ,, - 14 Scholar
Mary Craig - 70 Visitor

Thomas Lewis	- 19	Farm Labourer
John ,,	- 18	,, ,,
William Carter	- 18	,, ,,
Thomas Eavans	- 21	,, ,, d. 12/5/1948 aged 88
Thomas Bright	- 32	,, ,,
Elizabeth Bridgwater	- 17	Domestic servant
Hannah Speakes	- 15	Domestic servant

1891 Occupied by James Haynes

1894 182 acres let to Richard Wilding at £170 a year

1906 Occupied by Thomas William Gwilt

1911 Upper & Lower Moor-19½a-sold to Edward Martin Dunne
Ragbatch sold to Richard Wilding - 8 acres
Farm now 154 acres & valued at £3000 by Henry Russell & Son Shrewsbury.
T Gwilt still in occupation.

1920 J P Stanier sold to Helen Kate May of Church Moor, Church Stretton for £3200. Occupied by John Sydney and Ellen Edwards.

1924 H K May sold to Richard Roberts for £2800, who then occupied it.

1929 R Roberts died 25 March aged 60. Mrs Hannah Esther Roberts occupied it

1939 A Perkins was tenant and then, in 1947, he bought it for £4000.

1950 Glebe land - Upper & Lower Dol (20alr33p) bought for £400 and added to the farm acreage.

A further hundred yards down the lane is Lower or Ragdon Farm. This, too, is typical of the post-Elizabethan era, stone built with two staircases, one leading to the servants quarters and the other for the family. However, the architecture differs from the other farm, in that it is half-timbered with the stone, and is more in keeping with other farm houses in the area. In 1900 the house was considerably altered from the original to its present layout.

The Wilding family have farmed the land from around 1750. There is a story that the family lost the farm in a bet with Thomas Dunne at Bangor races. Whether or not this was true, the Dunne family certainly owned it until 1947 when John Wilding repurchased it.

Around 1800 Thomas Wilding was much involved in Parish life, being one of the Overseers of the Poor, as well as being a Church warden.

In 1843 the valuation of the 161 acres was a rent of £162. Some of the land was in odd parcels at Chelmick and in Chelmick Valley. In

Ragdon Farm

1852 Thomas married Mary Rogers from Upper Farm at Chelmick and they had four children. There were always six or seven servants living in. In 1861 the housemaid was Susan Duckett. Was she the sister of Sarah who was a Dairymaid at Upper Farm, Chelmick and may have been the girl who was reputed to have been murdered and who haunts the Ghost Hole?

The Thomas Wilding family all lived to ripe old ages. Thomas 76, Mary his wife 93, Richard (their son) 80, Sarah (daughter) 83 and Thomas (youngest son) 89.

The census returns from 1841-1881 show the two farms to house 23-25 people. Today there are but 7. How farming has changed. The workers in the old days were, in general, taken on at the Annual Hiring Fairs held on May 14 in Church Stretton. Some of the senior or more important workers would stay for several years, but none were ever employed for as long as 10 years, according to the census returns.

Ragdon Farm. The drawing below shows the house as it was before the roof was raised in 1900.

Neither farm was ever part of the Lutwyche or Hope Bowdler Estate, always being privately owned.

There is no record of there ever having been any farm worker's cottage at Ragdon.

RAGDON FARM - MAP No. 21.

1792 Reference to Mr Wilding of Ragdon in the Blacksmith's Day book.

1841 Census
Thomas Wilding - 25 Farmer
William ,, - 20 Agric Lab
Mary ,, - 25
Richard Chickley - 20 Agric Lab
John Davies - 20 ,, ,,
Thomas ,, - 13 ,, ,,
William Carter - 15 ,, ,,
Elizabeth Dodd - 20 Female servant
Francis Cole - 14 ,, ,,

1843 Valuation - 161 acres 0r 11p Estimated rental £162-3-2
Owned by Thomas Dunne Rateable value £148-12-0

1851 Census
Thomas Wilding - 35 Farmer m. 4/11/52 Mary Rogers
Mary ,, - 36 Sister m. 11/11/52 John Hyde, farmer
William Benbow - 24 Agric Lab
John Davies - 20 ,, ,,
Richard Edwards - 22 ,, ,,
Richard Williams - 19 ,, ,,
William Elsor - 15 ,, ,,
Ann Harvey - 18 Housemaid
Elizabeth Williams - 14 ,,

1861 Census
Thomas Wilding - 50 Farmer (160a)
Mary ,, - 35
Richard ,, - 7
Sarah ,, - 2
Susan Duckett - 20 Housemaid
Mary Eavans - 27 Dairymaid
John Jones - 29 Labourer
Edward Miles - 20 ,,
David Griffiths - 30 Carter
Hubert Jones - 14 Servant
William Fox - 13 ,,

1871 Census
Thomas Wilding - 60 Farmer (160a)
Mary ,, - 45
Richard ,, - 17 Sarah Wilding - 12
Margaret ,, - 9 Thomas ,, - 7

	Edna Lewis	- 16 Dairymaid
	Martha Morgan	- 15 General servant
	John Marston	- 22 Farm servant
	James Carter	- 21 ,, ,,
	George ,,	- 16 ,, ,,
	James Donnelly	- 14 ,, ,,
1881	Census	
	Thomas Wilding	- 73 Farmer (168a) d. 7/6/84 aged 76
	Mary ,,	- 56 d. 4/3/1919 aged 93 (Lt. S.)
	Richard ,,	- 27 d. 10/9/1943 aged 80 (Lt. S.)
	Sarah ,,	- 22 d. 28/7/1942 aged 83 (Lt. S.)
	Margaret ,,	- 19
	Thomas ,,	- 18 d. 3/5/1952 aged 89
	Benjamin Bowen	- 28 Indoor servant
	Richard Powell	- 25 Indoor servant
	Edward Cox	- 18 Servant
	John Corfield	- 21 ,,

The farm was subsequently occupied by Richard Wilding & Thomas Wilding.

1947 Bought by John and Bill Wilding.

Apart from the two farms referred to above there are today four other houses in Ragdon. A bungalow built by the Roberts family of Ragdon Manor Farm in 1929 at the far end of the Shop Leasow field. Another adjacent to the farm built in 1950 and Clemcroft built just before the Second World War, which is situated just before Hazler Hill.

The fourth property is Dryhill Farm which was included in Hope Bowdler Parish in 1968, previously being in Church Stretton.

Dryhill is built on the S.E. side of the Ragleth Hill and was originally 19 acres, later increased to 24. It was owned by Mrs. A. G. Coleman, the Lady of the Manor in Church Stretton, in the early 1800's and sold to Moses George Benson in 1851 when it then became part of the Hope Bowdler Estate.

The house is of stone and was built in the 1700's or even earlier. An interesting point is that it is marked on nearly every printed map, the earliest Ordnance Map in 1830 and those produced even earlier.

Although of small acreage it had individual hedged fields and was farmed with wheat and potatoes, as well as meadow land long before the Enclosure Act of the 1830's. The fields all have a tithe number, but no names, which is unusual as every other field on tithe maps carries a name.

Dryhill Farm, Ragdon. (above) as it was in 1895.

In 1861 no less than eleven people lived there (a two up and one down house) and two of them, the Jones brothers, were woodsmen. They were, incidentally, the grandfather and great uncle of Norman Jones who lives at Chelmick Pools.

At the time of the building of the railway - Shrewsbury to Hereford - in 1851/2, they used to carry potatoes down to Church Stretton from Dryhill and sell them to the Irish labourers working on the line for them to bake.

Thomas Carter lived and farmed the land for over twenty years until his death. Then, in 1883, it was farmed by Robert Haynes, along with the main Ragdon Manor Farm. By 1895 John Hughes, farmer and wheelwright, was living there with his family. Sadly, on January 14th 1895 his young son Charlie set out in winter, when the snow was very deep, to go to Hope Bowdler. He fell from his horse and was found dead.

One of his daughters, Mrs. Hubbard, was renowned in the area for her large pork pies that were cooked in the bread oven.

The family moved to a cottage in Chelmick Valley where the Cadwalladers had lived for well over fity years.

In 1921, when the Bowdler Estate was sold, John Jones of Acton Scott bought Dryhill for £355. He never lived there himself, and it was let to various tenants until his death in 1946.

DRYHILL FARM - MAP No. 21A.

1838 Owned by Mrs A G Coleman, 'Lady of the Manor' who owned a lot of property in Church Stretton. Thomas Downs in occupation.

1841 Census

Thomas Downs	- 65 Farmer
Ann ,,	- 50
Susan ,,	- 15
Caroline ,,	- 7 gd daughter

1851 Bought by R A Benson and increased to 24 acres 2r 0p
Census

Ann Downs	- 62 Widow
Caroline ,,	- 17 gd daughter, Agric Lab
Thomas Gwilliam	- 4 gd son of shoemaker
Thos Williams	- 18 Farm servant

1861	Census			
	Thomas Carter	- 41 Farmer (25a)		
	Mary ,,	- 38	Richard Carter	- 12
	Ann ,,	- 10	Mary ,,	- 8
	Jane ,,	- 4	John ,,	- 3
	Thomas ,,	- 3	Infant	- 2 days
	Edwin Jones	- 31 Labourer		
	Richard ,,	- 29 ,,		
1871	Census			
	Thomas Carter	- 51 Farmer & woodranger		
	Mary ,,	- 48	Richard Carter	- 22 Labourer
	John ,,	- 13	Thomas ,,	- 13
	Ellen ,,	- 9	Martin ,,	- 7
1881	Census			
	Thomas Carter	- 62 Farmer		
	Mary ,,	- 59		
	John ,,	- 23 Farmer's son		
	Thomas ,,	- 23 Labourer in woods		
	Martin ,,	- 17 ,, ,, ,,		

1883 Occupied by Robert Haynes of Ragdon

1905 Occupied by John & Jane Hughes, Farmer & wheelwright.

1917 Occupied by John Haynes

1921 Sold as part of Hope Bowdler Estate by G R Benson to John Jones of Action Scott for £355-14-6. Mr Jones never lived there.

Other occupants were the Bridgwater, Wardman and James families during the intervening years until:-

1946 Sold by William Cranage on behalf of John Jones dec'd to T E Morris for £490, 2nd October.

1953 Sold to Harold Musson for £2000, 15th October.

1959 Sold to G B Richards for £3000, 11th June.

1965 12 acres sold to Mrs T E Pope for £2200.

1975 6 acres and Hill rights for 50 sheep sold to Mrs M E Morris for £3500.

1976 Sold to A Dakers.

CHELMICK - PEOPLE & HOUSES

The other township in the Parish, Chelmick, can be approached by way of Sheffield Lane off the Ticklerton Road or by turning left at the top of Bull Lane out of Hope Bowdler.

Chelmick having many more houses than Ragdon appears more often in the Church records of various families. The Knott family around 1720 as farmers. Edward Porvis and Adam Griffiths are both listed as Yeomen along with Thomas Speake who certainly farmed there. A William Davies was a weaver there in 1725.

Chelmick is naturally divided into two parts - the two farms on the high ground and the cottages along the Valley.

Approaching from Ragdon, the first farm on the left is Upper Farm 129 acres and, in 1843, a rental of £124 4s 8d. It was farmed by the Rogers family throughout the 1800's.

It is obviously a very old farm, having been sold in 1623 to Viscount Lumley. By 1653 it formed part of the estate of Henry Smith of Shrewsbury who held the estate in Chelmick 'in trust for the benefit of the Poor of Shrewsbury' and later gave it into the possession of the Corporation of Shrewsbury who retained it until it was sold to William Davies. In 1653 the tenant was George Wilkes, paying an annual rent of £80 which, when compared with the 1843 rent of £124, seems to be high. The land, on the other hand, sold for £400 in 1623 increased six times in the 300 years until it was sold for £2,600 in 1942.

Upper Farm still has the original 17th century house and buildings, they may be even older or have been built on the site of an earlier dwelling. This may have been the home of the Phillips family who were mentioned as being "gentry of Chelmick". The oldest gravestone in Hope Bowdler Churchyard is dated 15 March 1657 Francis Philips of Chelmick aged 63. The stone has a skull and crossbones engraved on it.

In the Sale details of 1942 it is described as an old fashioned homestead, strongly constructed of stone with slated roof. An excellent water supply by gravitation from a spring and reservoir situated at Dryhill. There were four bedrooms approached by the main staircase with a separate staircase from the kitchen to two Staff bedrooms. The census returns show four or five workers living in.

Upper Farm, Chelmick. The house as it was in about 1900 (top) with Mrs Fanny Davies at the door and, as it is today, little altered in appearance over several hundred years.

UPPER FARM - CHELMICK - MAP No. 24.

1635 Sold by Thomas Chelmick to Viscount Lumley for £400

1653 Given to Shrewsbury Corporation for the benefit of the poor of Shrewsbury.

1841 Census
John Rogers - 50 Farmer
Elizabeth ,, - 50
Richard .. - 25 d. 10/2/43 aged 27
William ,, - 20 d. 20/6/43 aged 22
Margaret ,, - 18 d. 18/5/59 aged 36
Mary ,, - 15
John Ball - 15 Agric Lab
John Lewis - 10 ,, ,,

1843 Valuation - 129 acres 0r 15p Est. Rental £124-4-8
Rateable value £114-8-0

1851 Census
John Rogers - 64 Farmer (130a) d. 19/4/55
Elizabeth ,, - 62
John ,, - 30 Farmer's son employed
Mary ,, - 25 Farmer's daughter employed
m. 4/11/52 to Thomas Wilding
Eliza ,, - 23 m. 6/1/53 to Edwin Harley
Margaret Morris - 2 granddaughter
William Henry - 3 mths grandson
William Humphrey - 22 Agric Lab
Robert Morris - 18 ,, ,,
Joseph Benbow - 11 ,, ,,

1861 Census
Elizabeth Rogers - 74 Widow, farmer d. 2/9/64
John ,, - 40
Mary ,, - 35 wife of John
Elizabeth ,, - 6 Mary Jane Rogers - 5
John Meredith ,, - 1 William ,, - 10
Alice Emma ,, - 5 Granddaughter
Sarah Duckett - 19 Dairymaid
Charles Mount - 21 Carter
Samuel Sebrey - 17 Cowman
William Partin - 14 Ploughboy

1871 Census
John Rogers - 54 Farmer (130a)
Mary ,, - 46
Elizabeth ,, - 15 m. 4/12/77 to William Downes (Wine Merchant)
Mary Jane ,, - 13 m. 24/4/89 to C H Rogers, Farmer Ch. S.
John ,, - 11 d. 28/9/72
Richard & William ,, - 8

	Charles ,,	- 6
	Alfred ,,	- 1 d. 3/5/71 (scarlet fever & diptheria)
	Jane Lewis	- 13 Dairymaid
	Richard Jones	- 19 General servant
	George Lewis	- 18 ,, ,,
	Jane Rogers	- 63 Visitor
1881	Census	
	John Rogers	- 63 Farmer (130a) d. 3/2/93
	Mary ,,	- 56 d. 8/3/88 aged 62
	Mary ,,	- 23
	John ,,	- 21
	Charles ,,	- 14
	Charles Bridgwater	- 20 Servant

1905 William Davies was in occupation and it is probable that he bought the farm at around this time.

1942 William Davies (d. 2/12/1967 and Fanny d. 10/6/1949) sold the farm 125 acres 2r 11p plus 1 acre 0r 11p (in H.B.) for £2600 to Ellis Jones.

Chelmick Manor Farm

Chelmick Manor Farm is a stone built Elizabethan Manor House. The foundations are very much older, as it was the home of the Earl of Elmundewik back in the 11th century. The Chelmick family lived there in an unbroken line until 1635. Other owners or occupants were the Lloyds, Morralls and the Russells described in the Hope Bowdler records as "gentry of Chelmick".

The 1843 valuation show it as 128 acres with a rental of £118.

The house was probably empty for long periods during the 1800's as no census returns can be linked to it for 1841, 1851 or 1881. Certainly Martha Haynes of Ragdon Manor was farming the land in 1841 (earlier too?) and in 1851. John Faulkner was the tenant from

Chelmick Manor Farm. The left hand part of the house is of later construction and bears a date T R 1719. The older part of the house is said to have had its own private chapel and a secret cupboard. Much of the panelling was removed to Eaton Church around 1900.

1861 until about 1877 when he retired. In 1873 Wm. Hall sold the farm, along with several Chelmick Valley holdings to Thos. Berks. Turner. In the next few years a variety of people farmed it - Fred Hall, Richard and Mary Wilding, William Haynes, Herbert Jones and then in 1907 it was sold again and occupied by Ed Humphries. In 1918 it was sold yet again to the Davies family.

CHELMICK MANOR FARM - MAP No. 25.

1841 Census - uninhabited

1843 Valuation - 129a 3r 15p Estimated Rental £118-18-8
Rateable value £109-0-0

1851 Census - uninhabited

1861 Census

John Faulkner	- 41 Farmer (129a)		
Sarah ,,	- 36		
William ,,	- 15	Margaret Faulkner	- 14
John George ,,	- 12	Edward ,,	- 11
Sarah Ann ,,	- 10	Susannah ,,	- 9
Thomas ,,	- 7	Elizabeth ,,	- 4
Mary ,,	- 2		

1871 Census

John Faulkner	- 50 Farmer (124a) d. 26/11/1906 aged 86		
Sarah ,,	- 46 d. 7/10/76 aged 52		
Edward ,,	- 21	Thomas Faulkner	- 16
Elizabeth ,,	- 13	Mary ,,	- 12
Richard ,,	- 11	Louisa ,,	- 8
Frederick ,,	- 7	Edmund ,,	- 6
Hannah ,,	- 2	Richard Cox	- Farm servant
Alice ?	- 25 visitor, dressmaker		
Alice ?	- 2		
Fanny ?	- 8 mths		

1873 Sold on 30th July at the Railway Hotel, Church Stretton 127 acres 2r 12p together with 61 acres at Hatton Farm in the occupation of John Pinches and 6 Lots along Chelmick Valley.

1881 Census - uninhabited.

When the farmhouse was 'uninhabited' it is probable that Haynes of Ragdon Manor farmed the land.

The ownership of Chelmick Manor included, from 1843 to 1918 The Honourable Nugent, Rev John Morrall, Job Taylor and Thos Berks Turner.

1907 Sold on 18th July at the Bucks Head Hotel, Church Stretton 123 acres 2r 19p the property of the late Thos Berks Turner and 2 Lots at Chelmick Pools.

1918 Sold on 27th June (as 1907) at the Bucks Head. Albert Speke was in occupation.
Bought by George Davies, who died 5/11/1932 aged 76.

1934 Fred Davies was in occupation until 1963

1963 Bought, 9th September with 119 acres 2r 36p, by John Davies.

Opposite Chelmick Manor Farm are two semi-detached cottages which were occupied by agricultural labourers until, in the 1970's, it became a single dwelling with the outbuildings being used as a farrier's shop. In the mid-1980's it was extensively renovated.

Chelmick Cottage, originally semi-detached.

CHELMICK - semi-detached cottage - MAP No. 22.

1841 Census
John Price - 40 Agric Lab m. 17/5/26 Charlotte Reynolds
Charlotte ,, - 40
Ann ,, - 14 Mary Price - 11
Emma ,, - 9 Frederick Wellings - 5

1851 Census
Samuel Bennett - 77 Agric Lab d. 8/12/52
Sarah ,, - 81 d. 9/1/1859
Richard ,, - 59 Agric Lab
Betsy ,, - 50 Housemaid

1861 Census
John Cox - 33 Butcher
Fanny ,, - 29 William Cox - 7
Richard ,, - 4 Jane ,, - 4

1871 Census
Joseph Wilde - 53 widower, Agric Lab
Emma ,, - 18
Edwin ,, - 10
Francis ,, - 8

1881 Census
John Morgan - 73 Farm labourer
Ann ,, - 64 d. 20/4/92 aged 76
Edmund ,, - 29

CHELMICK - semi-detached cottage - MAP No. 23.

1841 Census
Ann Poston - 60 Agric Lab
Richard ,, - 30 ,, ,,
Sarah ,, - 20 Female servant

1851 Census
Ann Poston - 71 d. 15/8/59 aged 80
Richard ,, - 41 Agric Lab
Sarah ,, - 30 Housemaid

1861 Census
Richard Poston - 50 Labourer d. 22/5/1875 aged 65
Sarah ,, - 38

1871 Census - uninhabited

1881 Census
William Bridgwater - 28 Farm labourer
Ann ,, - 28
Herbert ,, - 4
Sarah ,, - 2
George ,, - 11 Scholar, William's brother

The cottage has now been modernised and made into a single dwelling.

Continuing down a steep hill one comes to Chelmick Pools and the Valley. This small valley is an interesting 18/19th century development. In some respects it is understandable being in a sheltered position and having a very good water supply. On the other hand it is isolated, not really being on the way to anywhere. It was a community of, mainly, farm workers, but it was some distance from Hope Bowdler village.

At the foot of the hill are the Chelmick Pools on the left, and behind them a house and buildings with three acres and a rental of £7 8s 7d. The Harley family lived there until 1874, by which time the land had been increased to nine acres. In 1881 it was uninhabited, but the cottage still existed, as it was included in the sales of Chelmick Manor Farm in 1907 and 1918 as a separate lot. A family called Bullock were the last to live in it until Mr Buddicom (who owned other land in the area) bought it and did away with the cottage.

CHELMICK POOLS Tithe No. 160 - MAP No. 26.

1841 Census
- William Harley - 50 Agric Lab m. 8/7/16 Ann Bridgman
- Ann ,, - 47
- John ,, - 23 Agric Lab
- William ,, - 18 ,, ,,
- Mary ,, - 12
- Thomas ,, - 9
- Edward ,, - 21 Agric Lab

1843 Valuation - 3a 1r 21p Est. Rental £7-8-7-
Owner - Hon Nugent. Rateable value £6-15-4

1851 Census
- William Harley - 60 Agric Lab d. 26/1/56 aged 65
- Ann ,, - 55
- John ,, - 33 Agric Lab
- William ,, - ,, ,,
- Mary ,, - 21 Servant
- Thomas ,, - 19 Cordwainer

1861 Census
- William Harley - 38 Labourer m. 12/11/68 Mary Goode
- John ,, - 44 Brother d. 2/8/71 aged 53
- Ann ,, - 67 Mother d. 19/7/71 aged 76
- Maria ,, - 45 Sister, unmarried, housekeeper, d. 1875 aged 60 Ch.S.

1871 Census
- William Harley - 44 Labourer d. 26/11/90 aged 67
- Mary ,, - 37 d. 26/12/72 aged 38
- Edwin Goode - 18
- Jane Goode - 15
- Mary Bullock - 70

1873 Sold as Lot 8 to Thos Berks Turner
1881 Census - uninhabited

Across the Pools, below the Old Quarry, was a cottage and two acres occupied by John Griffiths, a Mason, with a rent of £4 6s 9d. Henry Goode then lived there until his death in 1862 when Richard Jones moved in. He increased the land to fifteen acres and subsequently bought it, running a dairy farm, piggery and contract farm work with his sons. (See also under 'Farming' and 'People'). The Jones family lived there without break and today Norman Jones (Richard's grandson) lives in a modern bungalow built on the site of the original cottage which was burnt down in 1956.

From the cottage and in a nearby building, the Miss Jones ran tea rooms both before and after the Second World War. People used to come from all over the County and further afield, such was their renown. Many 'notable' people were among the visitors as men like Sir Ian Fraser of the St. Dunstan's Blind Association (who lived in Church Stretton) brought many friends there for a quiet afternoon tea.

The modern house built on the site of the Jones cottage

CHELMICK POOLS Tithe No. 166 - MAP No. 27.

1841	Census	
	John Griffiths	- 70 Mason d. 4/3/44 aged 78
	Mary ,,	- 69 d. 4/6/42 aged 69
	Elizabeth Goodman	- 13 Female servant
1843	Valuation - 2a 1r 35p Est. rental £4-6-9	
	Owner - Hon Nugent Rateable value £4-0-0	
1851	Census	
	Henry Goode	- 64 Pauper, Agric Lab m. 28/2/32 Ann Griffiths
	Ann ,,	- 49 d. 14/2/59
	Thomas ,,	- 13 d. 8/1/95 aged 57
	Betsy ,,	- 12
	John ,,	- 10 d. 12/3/52 aged 11
	William ,,	- 8

The original thatched cottage, Chelmick Pools.

1861	Census	
	Henry Goode	- 76 Labourer d. 9/12/62
	Mary ,,	- 27 Housekeeper m. 12/11/68 William Harley
	Edwin ,,	- 7
	Jane ,,	- 5
1871	Census	
	Richard Jones	- 38 Agric Lab
	Ann ,,	- 36
	Philemon ,,	- 8 d. 12/2/1947 aged 84
	Jasper ,,	- 4
	Katherine ,,	- 2
1873	Sold as Lot 7 to Thos Berks Turner	

The Miss Jones' Tea Rooms, Chelmick Pools. Note the bee hives in the garden.

1881	Census	
	Richard Jones	- 49 Farmer (15a) d. 21/3/1916 aged 83
	Ann ,,	- 44 d. 27/6/1913
	Jasper ,,	- 14 m. 27/6/1900 Louisa Rogers
	Katherine ,,	- 12
	Sarah ,,	- 10
	Emma ,,	- 7 m. 29/1/1913 A. Speke
	Clara ,,	- 5
	Mary ,,	- 2
	Fanny ,,	- 1
1907	Sold as Lot 2, occupied by P Jones	
1918	Sold as Lot 3, occupied by Jasper Jones	

Rev. Silvester Horne talking with Jasper Jones.

Across the road, on the left at the start of the track that runs the full length of the Valley was a large garden belonging to the Jones property. There, by 1881, a small 'one up one down' cottage had been built. This has since been drastically altered, enlarged and is lived in by the Barrett family.

No 1 Chelmick Valley (on the right). Chelmick House (on the left) built by Jasper Jones in 1930. Note the large cultivated garden along the length of the bank.

No. 1 CHELMICK VALLEY Tithe No. 168 - MAP No. 27A.

1843 Valuation - part of John Griffiths land

1873 Sold as Lot 9, occupied by Thos Goode but no house

1881 Census

William Reade		- (name not clear) - 36 Farm Labourer		
Marion	,,	- 41		
Charles	,,	- 13	Frederick ?	- 11
Charlotte	,,	- 2	Albert ,,	- 5
Edgar	,,	- 2	Agnes ,,	- 1

1918 Sold as Lot 2, occupied by Philemon & Jasper Jones

The road continues up the hill to join Sheffield (or Shuffles) Lane. At the top was a cottage with a rental of £3. The Miles family from Soudley bought it around 1920 and pulled the old cottage down. In its place they erected an old seaside bathing cabin which they had towed behind a lorry from Blundell Sands. The cabin was on a chassis with iron wheels and they had to stop at frequent intervals to grease the axles. (These wheels have recently been on sale at £150). The chassis still had the old horse shafts on the front. The cabin was erected on site in the 1930's, later being added to. It was demolished in 1984 and a new house built. The Roberts family were living there in 1881 and the last of them died in the Workhouse.

The old bathing cabin, now demolished and a modern house built on the site.

SHEFFIELD LANE Tithe No. 174 - MAP No. 29.

1841 Census

Edward Cadwallader - 30 Agric Lab m. 24/7/33 M Richards
Mary ,, - 30
Thomas ,, - 7
Samuel ,, - 3
Sarah ,, - 1

1843 Valuation - 2r 23p Estimated Rental £3-0-0
Owner - Hon Nugent Rateable value £2-10-0

1851 Census
Edward
Cadwallader - 40 Agric Lab, Pauper
Mary ,, - 40
Thomas ,, - 17 d. 26/11/1917 aged 87 (w/house)
Sarah ,, - 10 John Cadwallader - 9
George ,, - 6 Richard ,, - 3

1861 Census
John Roberts - 49 Labourer
Mary ,, - 65
William ,, - 25

1871 Census
John Roberts - 58 Agric Lab
Mary ,, - 74
William ,, - 35 Agric Lab

1881 Census
John Roberts - 69 Agric Lab
William ,, - 45 ,, ,, d. 17/2/1911 aged 72
in Union workhouse

Back along the Valley track was a small cottage with 3r 4p and a rent of £3. Although very small, it was divided into two and lived in by two families. The first part was never mentioned in any census return. Thos. Humphries lived in the other half. He lived there all his life until he died aged 88 in 1884. His wife died aged 70, and he had remarried a widow Margaret Banks, in 1876.

No. 2/3 CHELMICK VALLEY Tithe No. 171 - MAP No. 28.

1841 Census
Thomas
Humphries - 40 Agric Lab
Sarah ,, - 35
William ,, - 11 Elizabeth Humphries - 9
Thomas ,, - 5 d. 11/5/66 aged 30
Maria ,, - 1

1843 Valuation - 3r 4p Estimated Rental £3-0-0
Owner - Hon Nugent Rateable value £2-10-0

1851 Census
Thomas
Humphries - 53 Agric Lab
Sarah ,, - 48
Richard ,, - 8 d. 18/7/63 aged 20

No. 2/3 Chelmick Valley, now derelict.

1861	Census		
	Thomas Humphries	- 59	Labourer
	Sarah ,,	- 57	
	William ,,	- 1	
	Caroline Hughes	- 11	Servant
1871	Census		
	Thomas Humphries	- 71	Agric Lab m. 17/4/76 Margaret Banks (widow)
	Sarah ,,	- 67	d. 23/6/73 aged 70
	William ,,	- 10	
1881	Census		
	Thomas Humphries	- 85	Farm Labourer d. 15/3/84 aged 88
	Margaret ,,	- 60	

No. 4 Chelmick Valley - 'The Hermitage'.

Some 200 yards further along was another cottage which has an inscription on the wall '1809', but this and the other cottages along the Valley were almost certainly built earlier than this. It was occupied by Richard Cadwallader and then his son until 1891. Then John and Jane Hughes moved there from Dryhill in about 1910. John lived to 94, dying on May 20th 1939, and his wife Jane was 72 when she was buried on December 22nd 1921. Today the original cottage has been modernised and added to.

No. 4 CHELMICK VALLEY Tithe No. 175 - MAP No. 30.

1841 Census
Richard
Cadwallader - 62 Agric Lab
Alice ,, - 57
Richard ,, - 30 ,, ,,
George ,, - 20 ,, ,,

1843 Valuation - 3r 2p Estimated rental £3-0-0
Owner - Hon Nugent Rateable value £2-10-0

1851	Census	
	Richard Cadwallader	- 73 Agric Lab d. 5/8/53 aged 75
	Alice ,,	- 68 d. 6/12/58 aged 79
	George ,,	- 30 Agric Lab
	Eliza Sebrey	- 2 Gd Daughter
1861	Census - uninhabited	
1871	Census	
	R Cadwallader	- 60 Agric Lab
1881	Census	
	R Cadwallader	- 70 Agric Lab d. 27/5/91 aged 81

The Chelmick Valley cart-track to the Birtley Road.

Continuing along the track towards Birtley are two more small stone cottages. The first one with four acres and a rental of £6 17s 7d was uninhabited at the 1841 census, but had been lived in earlier by T. Griffiths 'Bucher of ye Quarry', perhaps related to John Griffiths of Soudley who was also a butcher. Later a wheelwright lived there. It was uninhabited in 1861, then Benjamin Colley, his wife and five children lived there until 1873 (when it was sold) and they moved to Soudley. Ben Colley worked as groom for the Benson family.

In 1881 Thomas Carter was living there. He was known as "Wisdom Tom" and he worked in timber for Richard Jones of Hope Bowdler. His wife did washing and worked for Harry Cox of Ticklerton's grandfather. The cottage then became derelict and a new house built on the site in 1985.

No. 5 CHELMICK VALLEY Tithe No. 185 - MAP No. 31.

1841 Census - uninhabited

1843 Valuation - 4a 0r 21p Estimated rental £6-17-7.
Owner - Hon Nugent. Rateable value £6-2-0
Occupier - Thomas Griffiths sometime referred to as 'Bucher of ye Quarry', d. 2/11/1850.

1851 Census
Humphrey Parry - 38 Wheelwright
Elizabeth ,, - 30
John ,, - 8 Mary Parry - 5 d. Dec/58 aged 13
George ,, - 3 Robert Poston - 28

1861 Census - uninhabited

1871 Census
Benjamin Colley - 38 Agric Lab d. 2/5/1900 aged 65
Ann ,, - 32 d. 5/1/1914
Catherine ,, - 9 m. 17/5/95 R. Blakemore, Carpenter
Emma ,, - 7 m. 1/2/87 G. Potten M/chester
Ellen ,, - 4
William ,, - 2
Eliza ,, - 9 mths m. 13/8/1901 Abel Jones

1873 Sold as Lot 6, Charles Hughes in occupation.

1881 Census
Thomas Carter - 60 Labourer
Martha ,, - 53 Marion Carter - 15
Charles ,, - 12 William ,, - 3
Mary Pritchard - 23 Boarder

Thomas and Martha Carter - 'Wisdom Tom'.

No. 6 Chelmick Valley - derelict.

Fifty yards on, with three acres and a rental of £5 18s 7d, was another tiny cottage where Martha Morgan and her sister Mary lived. Martha was listed as an Agricultural labourer at 55, and when she was 75 as a pauper. By 1861 Richard Wilkes, a shoemaker, lived there, with a journeyman shoemaker, George Poole, and later his son Stephen worked with him. In 1873, when the cottage was sold, it appears the Wilkes family had left, as George Poole was listed as the Occupant. The 1881 census shows it as uninhabited and it became derelict.

No. 6 CHELMICK VALLEY Tithe No. 186 - MAP No. 32.

1841 Census
Martha Morgan - 55 Agric Lab
Mary ,, - 50

1843 Valuation - 3a 2r 13p Estimated rental £5-18-7
Owner - Hon Nugent Rateable value £5-6-0
Occupier - Ann Richards

1851	Census	
	Mary Morgan	- 75 Pauper, charwoman d. 8/1/58 aged 80
	George ,,	- 16 Idiot
1861	Census	
	Richard Wilkes	- 47 Shoemaker
	Eliza ,,	- 38 Stephen Wilkes - 7
	Mary Ann ,,	- 5 John George ,, - 3
	George Poole	- 20 Journeyman shoemaker
1871	Census	
	Richard Wilkes	- 57 Shoemaker
	Eliza ,,	- 48 d. 7/4/97
	Stephen ,,	- 17 Shoemaker
	Mary ,,	- 13
	John ,,	- 13
1873	Sold as Lot 5, George Poole in occupation	
1881	Census - uninhabited	

Across the Birtley road and just within the Parish boundary was a house and croft with 1 acre 2r 21p and a rental of £4 11s 0d. Edward Mason lived there until his death, aged 77, in 1865. There is, however, a slight mystery in that on 27th May 1847 there is a record of "Hire of horse and cart to convey Edward Mason, wife and two children to the Workhouse. The woman and family stated to be unable to walk from illness - 5s 0d." This was probably to the Union Workhouse in Church Stretton built in 1838. Before this the Hammond farmhouse, Hatton, had been the Parish workhouse. If, as is likely, this is the same family, the children would have been Ann, 4 years and William, 1 year and, presumably, in time they were able to leave the Workhouse and move back. When Ann was 22 she married Philip Croxton and, after her father's death, lived there until 1873 when it was sold. Philip Croxton was Estate carpenter for many years, then moved north of Shrewsbury to Grillshall where an example of his work still exists today - an oak fence, all pegged, with all the lower part of the posts burnt or charred. Edwin Harley (from 26) was living there in 1881 and he died in 1911 aged 84.

The house has been occupied at all times and today is still very much in its original state, although the Parrys have incorporated the outbuildings as part of the main house.

Wimmerfield, at the Birtley end of Chelmick Valley. (above) the original cottage and (below) as it is today after conversion and additional rooms.

CHELMICK VALLEY Tithe No. 190 - MAP No. 33.

1841	Census		
	Edward Mason	- 45	Agric Lab m. 24/7/32 (widower)
	Alice ,,	- 32	Alice Cadwallader
	Mary Poston	- 64	Agric Lab
	Daniel ,,	- 24	,, ,,
1843	Valuation - 1a 2r 21p Estimated rental £4-11-0		
	Owner - Hon Nugent Rateable value £4-0-0		
1851	Census		
	Edward Mason	- 65	Agric Lab
	Alice ,,	- 40	d. 26/4/56 aged 45
	Ann ,,	- 8	
	William ,,	- 5	
1861	Census		
	Edward Mason	- 73	Labourer d. 25/8/65 aged 77
	Ann ,,	- 19	m. 9/2/64 Philip Croxton
	William ,,	- 15	d. 9/4/77 aged 33 from tetanus following amputation of a hand torn in a machine.
1871	Census		
	Philip Croxton	- 30	Wheelwright
	Ann ,,	- 28	
	Mary ,,	- 9	George Croxton - 6
	Charles ,,	- 4	Emma ,, - 2
1873	Sold as Lot 4, Philip Croxton in occupation		
1881	Census		
	Edwin Harley	- 50	Labourer d. 29/7/1911 aged 84
	Elizabeth ,,	- 15	
	Margaret ,,	- 10	Scholar
	Christine ,,	- 7	

There was just one further dwelling located in a triangular piece of ground beside the footpath that runs from the Valley track up to the top of Sheffield Lane. This was the 'hovel'. This is the only reference to a hovel in the Parish records, although there were several listed for Church Stretton at the same period. It was a crude structure made out of branches, with the walls and roof interwoven with straw or bracken to keep out the weather. For some twenty years from 1841 Joseph Moile and his wife lived there. In 1861 it was not referred to in the census, but by 1871 John Sebrey, his wife and four children lived there and the burial register shows the death of two other children, one aged seven months and the other two days. A photograph of the hovel as it was in 1890 still exists, and it is quite incredible to think that anyone could actually live there, let alone bring up a family of four children. Although the piece of ground can still be identified there are not, of course, any other remains.

HOVEL - adjacent to Sheffield Lane - MAP No. 34.

1841	Census	
	Joseph Moile	- 41 Agric Lab
1851	Census	
	Joseph Moile	- 59 Agric Lab
	Mary ,,	- 58
1861	Census - uninhabited	

'The Hovel' - photographed by Miss Lilian Buddicom in 1890. It was still being lived in at that time!

1871	Census		
	John Sebrey	- 41	Agric Lab. M. 23/4/49 Ann Cadwallader
	Ann ,,	- 42	d. 24/8/98 in The Asylum, Bicton
	Elizabeth ,,	- 11	
	Emma ,,	- 8	
	Hannah ,,	- 4	
	Louisa ,,	- 1	
1881	Census		
	John Sebrey	- 50	Farm Labourer d. 21/3/1903 aged 73
	Robert Poston		Boarder, farm labourer

John Sebrey outside his hovel.

POST-1900

The main part of this book is concerned with the period before 1900, but it is necessary to make brief comment on the last 80 years, in addition to that covered in earlier chapters, to complete the Parish record.

The water supply to the houses in Hope Bowdler village was from springs and wells until a bore hole was put in at Manor Farm and used to supplement the supply as the number of houses and the general usage of water increased. Mains water was finally laid on in 1971/2.

Houses in Chelmick Valley depended on springs and the stream that ran through the Valley from the Pools. Some houses are now on mains supply. The farms and cottages at Chelmick depended on wells and spring water carried by pipe from Dryhill farm from the end of the 19th century, until the mains was laid on in 1980.

There is no mains supply to the houses on Hazler Hill or at Ragdon, springs or bore holes being the only source.

The 34 houses built in the 1800's or earlier have been commented upon earlier in the book, as have some of the modern houses built on the sites of those that became derelict.

The remainder of today's 63 houses is made up as follows:

1. Opposite the old Toll House, two bungalows.
2. On Hazler Hill, built in the 1930's, two bungalows, one of which was largely constructed from the old cricket pavilion of the Blue Bird Toffee sports ground near Dudley - costing just £15!
3. A wooden house at the top of Snatchfield bridlepath built for the Misses Walker just before the last war.
4. Two bungalows at Ragdon Manor Farm, one opposite the turning from Ragdon to Chelmick and the other near the farm house.
5. In Chelmick there is a bungalow across the road from Upper Farm and another built in 1983 for the farrier, between Upper and Chelmick Manor Farmhouses.
6. On the Soudley road, towards Hope Bowdler, on the right is a bungalow built in 1945.
7. At the bottom of Bull Lane are six houses built in the 1930's, and further up is Nethersprings, built in 1921. Further on, on a site where an old railway carriage stood, a bungalow was erected in 1982.

8. In the village between the old carpenter's shop and the Croxton's house is a bungalow, and across the road on the left of the Wenlock Road beyond Upper House farmhouse, two houses were built in 1980. Then come the twelve council houses, six built in the 1950's, two during the last war and the further four in the 1930's as agricultural workers' houses.
9. The most recent additions, in 1984/5, are the three conversions of the old Manor Farm barns into houses.

A Hope Bowdler village gathering 27th October 1956 to celebrate 3rd prize in the Wellington Journal 'Tidiest Village Competition'.

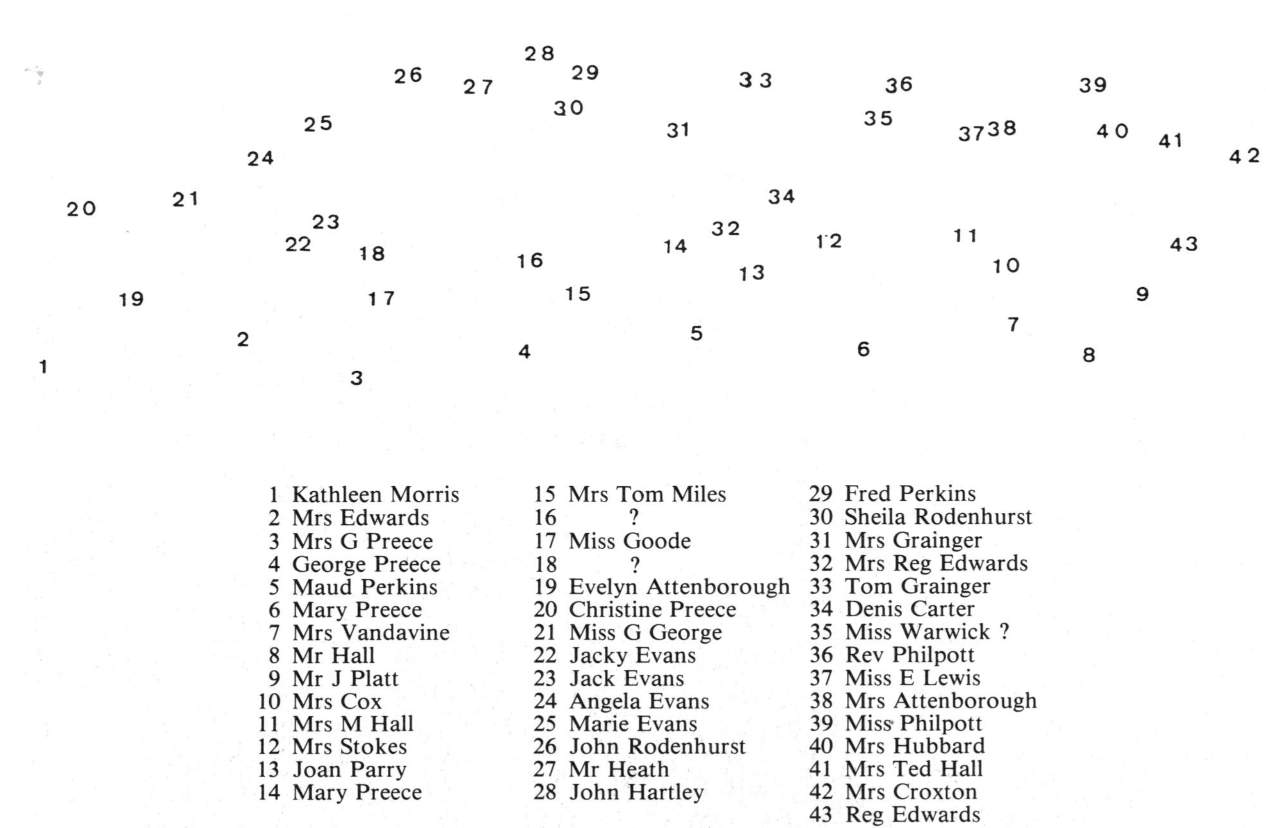

1 Kathleen Morris
2 Mrs Edwards
3 Mrs G Preece
4 George Preece
5 Maud Perkins
6 Mary Preece
7 Mrs Vandavine
8 Mr Hall
9 Mr J Platt
10 Mrs Cox
11 Mrs M Hall
12 Mrs Stokes
13 Joan Parry
14 Mary Preece
15 Mrs Tom Miles
16 ?
17 Miss Goode
18 ?
19 Evelyn Attenborough
20 Christine Preece
21 Miss G George
22 Jacky Evans
23 Jack Evans
24 Angela Evans
25 Marie Evans
26 John Rodenhurst
27 Mr Heath
28 John Hartley
29 Fred Perkins
30 Sheila Rodenhurst
31 Mrs Grainger
32 Mrs Reg Edwards
33 Tom Grainger
34 Denis Carter
35 Miss Warwick ?
36 Rev Philpott
37 Miss E Lewis
38 Mrs Attenborough
39 Miss Philpott
40 Mrs Hubbard
41 Mrs Ted Hall
42 Mrs Croxton
43 Reg Edwards

MEDIAEVAL HISTORY

Any records for this period for such a small community are, to say the least, conspicuous by their absence. Nevertheless, the Domesday Book is the first inventory of the people and assets of England, surveyed in 1085. Unlike the Tithe apportionment manuscripts and maps of 1843, the Domesday Book was not a record of individual owners, tenants, fields and rents in lieu of Tithes to the Church, but intended as a list of taxable assets from which William the Conqueror could levy his taxes and also for him to know the extent of his winnings. Or was it meant to be a definitive statement about a whole range of other features of every piece of land in England - something in the nature of an Estate Agent's inventory on a grand scale? Today the question remains not only undecided but academic.

By the year AD 1000 most of England was already divided into shires, which remained more or less the same until the reorganisation of county boundaries in 1974. The compilation of the Domesday information recorded all the lands held by the King and by his tenants, and of the resources which went with those lands. It also recorded which manors rightfully belonged to which estates. It also gave the identities of the tenants-in-chief (landholders) who held their lands directly from the Crown, and of their tenants and under-tenants. He was also able to know how much land his Archbishops and Bishops had and how much money it was all worth. At the time of Domesday 17% of the land was owned by the King, 26% by the Bishops and Abbots, and 54% by tenants-in-chief. The fact that the whole scheme was executed within two years displayed an incredible feat of organisation and showed the formidable will of William the Conqueror.

In each case the catalogue of lands begins with that held directly by the King, then (1) who held the land before the Conquest, (2) a description of the land, with the number and status of the inhabitants, number of ploughs, mills, etc. and the proportion of land held directly by the lord ('in demesne'), and (3) the value of the land in the time of Edward the Confessor (T.R.E. Tempus regis Edwardi) and now - that is in 1086.

Hope Bowdler (FORDRITISHOPE) and Chelmick (ELMUND-EWIC) are both entered in Domesday Folio 258 Book 2. There is no reference to Ragdon by name.

The two entries read:-

Chelmick - "HUGH FITZ-TURGIS hold of ROGER the EARL ELMUNDEWIC. EDRIC SAUVAGE held it with i berewick. Here iiii Hides geldable. The land is for vi oxteams. Here ix villeins have iii terms. In time of King Edward it was worth 12/- now 8/-. It was waste."

Hope Bowdler - "The same HUGH (Fitz-Turgis) holds FORDRITISHOPE. Edric Sauvage held it. Here iii Hides geldable. The land is for vi oxteams. In demesne are ii teams and iiii serfs ii female serfs and ii villeins with i team. There are two leagues of wood. In the time of King Edward it was worth 25/- now 15/-."

Note:- a 'BEREWICK' was an outlying estate dependent upon the chief manor. a 'HIDE' was a variable unit of area of land, enough for a household or around 120 acres and represents a family holding. 'GELDABLE' - taxable.
a 'VILLEIN' was a free villager, a serf, free in relation to all but his lord and not absolutely a slave.
a 'DEMESNE' was the portion of a manor which the holder worked as a home farm, with the help of labour due from the peasants. a 'HUNDRED' originated in 100 hides (12,000 acres) but this is not always strictly the case.

Edric Sauvage had been the Saxon tenant but the two hamlets are entered as being in different Hundreds. Hope Bowdler was in the Hundred of Culveston. This Hundred continued until the time of Henry I (1100-1135) when most of the manors were transferred to Munslow. Chelmick was in the Hundred of Lenteurde which straggled into what is now Radnorshire. It evidently gave its name to Leintwardine. However, its identity was soon lost and Chelmick was merged into Hope Bowdler. The Hundreds remained an important social unit until well into the 19th Century.

Edric Sauvage (so named by the Normans) is the Wild Eric celebrated in Shropshire Folklore. He is said to sleep in a cave under the Stiperstones, emerging whenever national disaster threatens, to ride his wild horses across the sky. He is also supposed to have married a fairy. In actual fact he led a revolt against the Normans and besieged Shrewsbury. His land and most of the surrounding districts were laid waste as a reprisal.

Ticklerton (Tickelevorde) was in the Domesday Hundred of Patinton and was transferred to Wenlock in the time of Henry I. Thus all three hamlets were in different Hundreds under early Norman administration. In the time of King Edward, the manor (of Ticklerton) was worth 100/- now 50/- (in 1086), quite clearly a much more valuable manor than the combined total of the other two. However, its value has depreciated very much, so it probably suffered the same devestation, though it did not belong to Edric.

The Domesday Book showed the Shropshire estates were small, none being more than 20 hides. Ticklerton with 10 hides was average, whilst Hope Bowdler and Chelmick with 3 hides each seem to have been too small to remain economic units and it was no surprise that the berewick of Chelmick was absorbed into Hope Bowdler. The berewick was most probably Chelmick Manor Farm.

Forty years after Domesday, Henry I (1126) gave the Honour of Montgomery to Baldwin de Bollers and the combined Manors of Fordritishope and Elmundewic (the berewick of Elmund) constituted a fief (land held in fee or on condition of military service) of one Knight's fee in that Honour.

Hope Bowdler derived its modern name from Baldwin de Bollers, the original name of Hope Bollers or Buhlers gradually developed into today's name.

By 1226 Hope Bowdler was the principal estate of Stephen de Bollers but he, somewhat confusingly, then took his name from the village and became known as Stephen de Hope.

At this time, the Priory at Much Wenlock was very powerful and Eaton, Harton, Ticklerton, Longville and Wolverton were all within its parish. Hope Bowdler, on the other hand, came under the Abbey at Buildwas.

Stephen de (or le) Hope was continually feuding with the Prior at Wenlock. At the Assizes of 1226, Stephen le Hope and three others were found to have disseized (deprived of an Estate) the Prior of his free tenement at Tykelworthin. Damages of 12/- were awarded. Two of the sureties were Robert de Raggedon and Adam de Chelmundewyk.

In a law suit of 1256 the records show "In 40th of Henry II (1256) the parson of Hope Bullers impleaded the Prior of Wenlock for rights in the Prior's wood of Sutley (Soudley). The Prior said that Stephen le Hope had disseized him of the said woods 25 years previously. A verdict was granted to the Prior." Stephen le Hope had been Patron of the Church of Hope Bowdler in 1231 - the earliest record of the existence of a church there.

In 1237 Nicholas, a parson of Hope Bowdler, was witness to an agreement of John de Raggedon to provide one foot soldier to do ward for fifteen days at Montgomery Castle. This is evidence that Ragdon was included in the manor of Chelmick referred to in 1126 as part of the Knight's fee in the Honour of Montgomery given to Baldwin de Bollers.

This provision of a foot soldier is an interesting sidelight on the feudal system and illustrates how inefficient the mustering of a feudal guard must have been. Ragdon is some thirty miles from Montgomery and presumably other local landowners would be fulfilling their obligations at the same time, so that a small force of men could travel together. This would have been repeated every fortnight, so the administration involved in maintaining a guard must have been formidable.

It appears that Stephen de Bollers died in 1255. His heir was under the wardship of Prince Edward as the Honour of Montgomery was in his custody. At the Inquisition (judicial enquiry) held upon his death, an Esheator (an official who watched over the property that falls to the feudal lord or to the state for want of an heir) was appointed to look after the escheats or fines due to the King and he then sent a writ to summon a jury to enquire what property a man had at the time of his death.

At this enquiry it was revealed that the Abbot of Buildwas held Raggedon, which contained one hide, as a gift of Robert de Acton. In 1291 the Abbot had 18/- assized rent and 2/- perquisites in Hope Bowdler. In the same year, Richard de Wilderley, who was now Lord of the Manor of Hope Bowdler, was engaged in litigation regarding land at Ragdon (presumably against the Abbot). The case was heard at Gloucester - the outcome is not known.

In 1291, the year of Pope Nicholas taxation, Edward I was allowed one tenth of clerical income. For Hope Bowdler this was £4-15-4, whereas it was £10 for Eaton. This is an early example of the relatively poor standing of Hope Bowdler vis-a-vis the other parishes in the neighbourhood.

A little earlier, in the first year of the reign of King Edward I (1272) George de Cantelupe held Hope Bowdler by Knight's service under the Barony of Montgomery and was adjudged to have free warren in this manor, with the liberty of a fair and market, both granted by the King. (It is unlikely that these were ever held).

At the end of the century Philip Burnel was adjudged to have all the rights granted to de Cantelupe earlier. Later, the Manor was carried in marriage by an heiress of the Burnels to John, Lord Lovel in whose family it continued until 1488 when Francis, Lord Viscount Lovel was slain on 16th June at the Battle of Stoke, Newark-on-Trent.

In 1240 William, son of William de Chelmundewyk, otherwise called William Erduff (? a Saxon name) was a tenant under Stephen le Hope. This particular William left his body for burial in the Abbey at Buildwas and bequeathed a ½ virgate of land in Hope Bowdler to the Abbey. (A virgate was a ¼ hide or about 30 acres).

Without doubt the 'Chelmick' family was an important one in the land and the family Arms were 'Vest. Three lions rampant guardant or. The crest is a lion sejant guardant or resting the dexter paw on a shield vert'.

In 1397, Richard Chelmick was the King's Squire and was among the Shropshire Knights who condemned Arundel, Archbishop of Canterbury, then banished by Richard II. In 1398 he was received into the fraternity of Lilleshall Abbey, at the same time John of Gaunt and his wife Catherine were also received into the fraternity after he fell ill following the Shrewsbury Parliament in Janury - he spent two days at the Abbey recuperating. Robert Chelmick was also Steward of the County of Cornwall.

In 1565 on 8th February Alice Chelmyche married a Thomas Lewis in Hope Bowdler church and, in 1574 on 29th January, Mary daughter of William Chelmych was baptised, then followed Thomas 12th November 1580, Joan 12th June 1582, Edwin 10th September 1584 and John 8th December 1585. On 18th July 1585 'the daughter' presumably either Mary or Joan, was buried. William was buried on 27th June 1604.

The Herald's Visitation of Shropshire in 1623 set out to trace and register the more influential people in the district. It was an idea of James I to raise money for the Exchequer. Gentry, who thought they had a right to a Coat of Arms, appeared before Clarenceaux or Norroy, King at Arms, at a certain place on a certain day in order that their pedigree might be duly received and their right to arm established. Fees were 25/- for a gentleman, 35/- for an Esquire and 55/- for a Knight or Baronet. The pedigree of the Chelmick family given in the Herald's Visitation of 1623 lists the family name through many generations as Chelmundwyk, Chelmedwick, Chelmewyke, Chelmewyche and Chelmick.

Ragdon is not specifically mentioned in Domesday Book records, it would have formed part of the Domesday Hundred of Lenteurde (Leintwardine) and been part of the hold of Roger the Earl Elmundewic (later called Chelmick) with iii hides geldable (taxable and a hide being around 120 acres and representing a family holding) within i berewick (an outlying estate dependent on the Chief Manor, probably Chelmick) and ix villeins (free villagers).

The earliest record of Ragdon occurs in 1202-3 when it was the fee of Richard de Wilderley, from whom it passed to the Hodnets. The mesne tenant was Robert de Laye (c1224-7) whose son, being clericus (clergyman) was known as Robert, Clerk of Acton. In 1237 he was acting as Deputy Sheriff to John le Strange of Knolyn, who was prominent in the King's service, being at one time Sheriff of Hampshire. His son, Hama le Strange, was granted the Manor of Stretton en le Dale on 21st February 1267.

Between 1245 and 1255 Robert, as son of Robert de Laye, gave Buildwas Abbey all his lands at Raggedone in pure alms, with all his common rights to the Manor of Hope, reserving a due which lay upon that portion of the premises held by John de Ragdon (i.e. tenant of a mesne tenant) to provide a foot soldier to do ward for 15 days at Montgomery Castle.

In 1253, before the Inquisition of 1255, Ragdon (1 hide) was held by the Abbot of Buildwas, while Odo de Hodnet did suit to the county and to the Munslow Hundred for both Ragdon and Hope. It is believed that Odo de Hodnet had acquired the mesne interest of Stephen le Hope in Ragdon, so that the total area of Ragdon should read 1⅓ hides and 1 virgate (about 200 acres).

In 1291, Richard de Wilderley was Lord of the Manor at Hope Bowdler and he was engaged in litigation regarding land at Ragdon. John de Ragdon and de Wilderley were almost certainly ancestors of the present Wilding family at Ragdon.

There was a great famine in England in 1315-16. Agriculture was in a very depressed state and tenants were in the unusual position of pleading not to be saddled with any more land. Money was beginning to take over from the original payment-in-kind of the feudal system.

In 1341 the Taxation of the Ninths was levied throughout the country to enable Edward III to continue the French wars. Because of the continued poverty and distress in the area, Hope Bowdler could not pay its full dues and was taxed only £1-6-8 instead of £4-15-4 because of "the mountainous nature of the district, the poverty of the tenants and a murrain or pestilience among the sheep". Shropshire and Herefordshire wool was fetching a very high price, so the sheep disease seems to have been very local.

The population of England probably numbered around five million at this time, and although there was a general increase in prosperity in trade, village life was apalling. A description from 'The English Village' reads:-

> "What passed for villages were agglomerations of filthy hovels, whose inhabitants wore the same threadbare collection of rags for months on end, had bodies which crawled with vermin, who drank from the streams that served their cattle and pigs, and whose huts were havens for rats, fleas and lice. Nine-tenths of the population lived thus, and most of the remainder lived in towns which at their biggest and worst were congested stinking death traps in which any disease could spread quickly and disastrously. These people did not seek to live in filth, but they possessed neither the means to avoid it, nor the knowledge of its consequences. They believed that mice appeared spontaneously in bags of flour, that cheese and not the fly gave birth to maggots and that disease could be caught by speaking its name. For living in conditions of squalor and ignorance, they paid a steady contribution to the graveyard."

The life, as described above, was doubtless accepted with mediaeval resignation and while they were familiar with disease, fire and famine as natural adversaries, the cruellest onslaught of all, the Black Death, struck in 1348. It delivered a crippling blow to the whole country and there is ample evidence of the decimating effect on the population of Shropshire.

Bubonic plague originated in Northern India, then spread outwards along land and sea trading routes across the Middle East and Europe. It was carried by the black or house rat. Port towns were the first to suffer, but merchants, travellers and trade goods soon spread it to the villages by fleas in clothes which would otherwise, as immobile populations, probably have been spared. Once it arrived in the agricultural holdings with grain stores and hovel dwellings already supporting a seething rat population, the plague was fearfully effective. Most peasant rooms were open to the rafters, and from rats - alive or dead - in the thatch, fleas could drop freely on the people huddled below. Estimates of one in five of the population being killed are recorded, yet there were some areas that escaped unscathed.

The distress, poverty and general low level of farming in the area was continuous for the majority of the 14th and 15th centuries too.

In spite of the proximity to the Welsh Border, there is no indication from the 13th and 14th century records to link the district with major political unrest or disturbance, but from earlier records it was evident that villages in the area had been laid waste. The region had been unsettled and inhabitants would not have put much effort into building houses throughout the time of this Welsh feuding and raiding.

Appendix No. 1

APPORTIONMENT OF THE RENT-CHARGE IN LIEU OF TITHES

On 23rd March 1843, Charles Howard of York, an Assistant Tithe Commissioner awarded the sums to be paid by way of Rent charge in lieu of Tithes in the Parish of Hope Bowdler in respect of land cultivated as follows:-

Arable -	763 acres 3r 14p
Meadow & Pasture -	567 ,, 3r 33p
Hill/Common of Pasture -	400 ,, 0r 0p
	1731 acres 3r 7p

The total annual sum to be paid to the Rector being £271-17£6 which had a value in Imperial Bushels of:-

225.87 of Wheat at 7s 0¼ per bushel
400.63 of Barley at 3s 11½ per bushel
576.67 of Oats at 2s 9 per bushel

SUMMARY

Landowners	*Total Quantities*	*Total Rent Charge*
	a r p	£ £ d
Ralph Benson, Esq.	998 24	112 13 0
John Broom	28	
Bezaleel Croxton	33	
Shrewsbury Charities	130 9	24 1 6
Thomas Dunne	164 3 35	29 4 0
Honble Nugent	146 1 17	25 10 0
Mrs Stackhouse	29 3 9	4 5 0
John Stanier, Esq.	178 1 9	34 4 0
Rev Geo Marsh, Glebe	45 3 29	8 0 0
	1,693 3 33	237 17 6
Roads	7 2 36	
	1,701 2 29	

The Valuation was carried out by Wm Wyley of Wellington.

The old field numbers for the Hope Bowdler Estate, before the Tithe Awards, are given in the left hand column, the corresponding details for Ragdon and Chelmick are not available.

Cow Pasture
Brick Kiln Leasow
Crown Top
Heley Leasow
Marsh
Garrotts Pool
Marsh
Hangings Piece
Hangings Piece
Pages Ground
Line
Coles Wood
Coles Wood
Line
Broomy Field
Coppice
Snatch Field
Snatch Field
Snatch Field
Plock
Hazler Land
Hazler Land
Rhaglith Wood
Rhaglith Wood
Wood
Plocks
Plantation
Lower Plocks
Coppice
Plantation
Plantation
Upper Plocks
Hazler Plantation
Rough Field
Field
Rhaglith Hill
Hazler Hill
Hill Field
Hill Field
Hill Field
The Shop Leasow
Dry Hill
Inclosure
Inclosure
Ox Pasture
Quarry Leasow
Quarry Leasow
Big Cold Hill
Hazler Field
Broomy Leasow
Cainall
Hazler Close
Butchers Leasow
Near Marrols
Piece above Road
Further Dales
Near Dales
Cow Pasture
Far Cross Field
Near Cross Field
Sideland Cold Hill
Lower Cainall
Little Chockery Field
The Stocking
Near Ditch Field
The Old Yard
Near Old Field
Colliers Yard
Barn Yard
Meadow
Upper Dol
Spring Piece
Spring Coppy
Little Cold Hill
Lower Stocking
Moors
The Moors
The Moors
Ragdon
The Yard Head
Ryegrass Piece
Garden Meadow
Stackyard Meadow
The Hearne
Lower Dol
Upper Feg Field
Lower Feg Field
Sheep Pasture
Upper Moor
The Little Moors
Barn Yard
Ditch Cop
Further Ditch
Ditch Cop
Bradley Furlong
The Sleeve
Quarry Leasow
Lower Moor
The Pine Furlong
Sidelend Meadow
Backside Leasow
Backside
Vetch Stubble
The Little Backside
Knowle Stock
Little Biglow Field
Biglow Field
Rag Batch
Further Broad Leasow
Broad Yard
Further Yard
Chelmick
Backside Field
Quarry
Pool or Moor Leasow
Briery Leasow
Far Brotches
The Brotches
Upper Hatch
Pike Meadow
Broad Meadow
Barn Yard
Lower Leasow
Upper Mill Leasow
Little Cote Leasow
Upper Chelmick
Hatch Meadow
The Big Cote Leasow
Lower Brotches
Brotch Coppice
The Pikes
Hill Headlands
Goodlong Meadow
Turnip Leasow
Lower Chelmick
Tinkers Meadow
The Coppy Piece
The Old Lands
Cow Pasture with Road
The Upper Little Saplings
The Spouts
The Pikes
The Big Saplings
The Lower Saplings
The Spawns
From Halton

Tithe Map 1843

Hope Bowdler Parish (part Church Stretton)

LOT IV.
Hope Bowdler Estate
Fm. Church Stretton
Fm. Cheimick & Ragdon
Gate
Township
Parish of Church Stretton
Township of Cholm

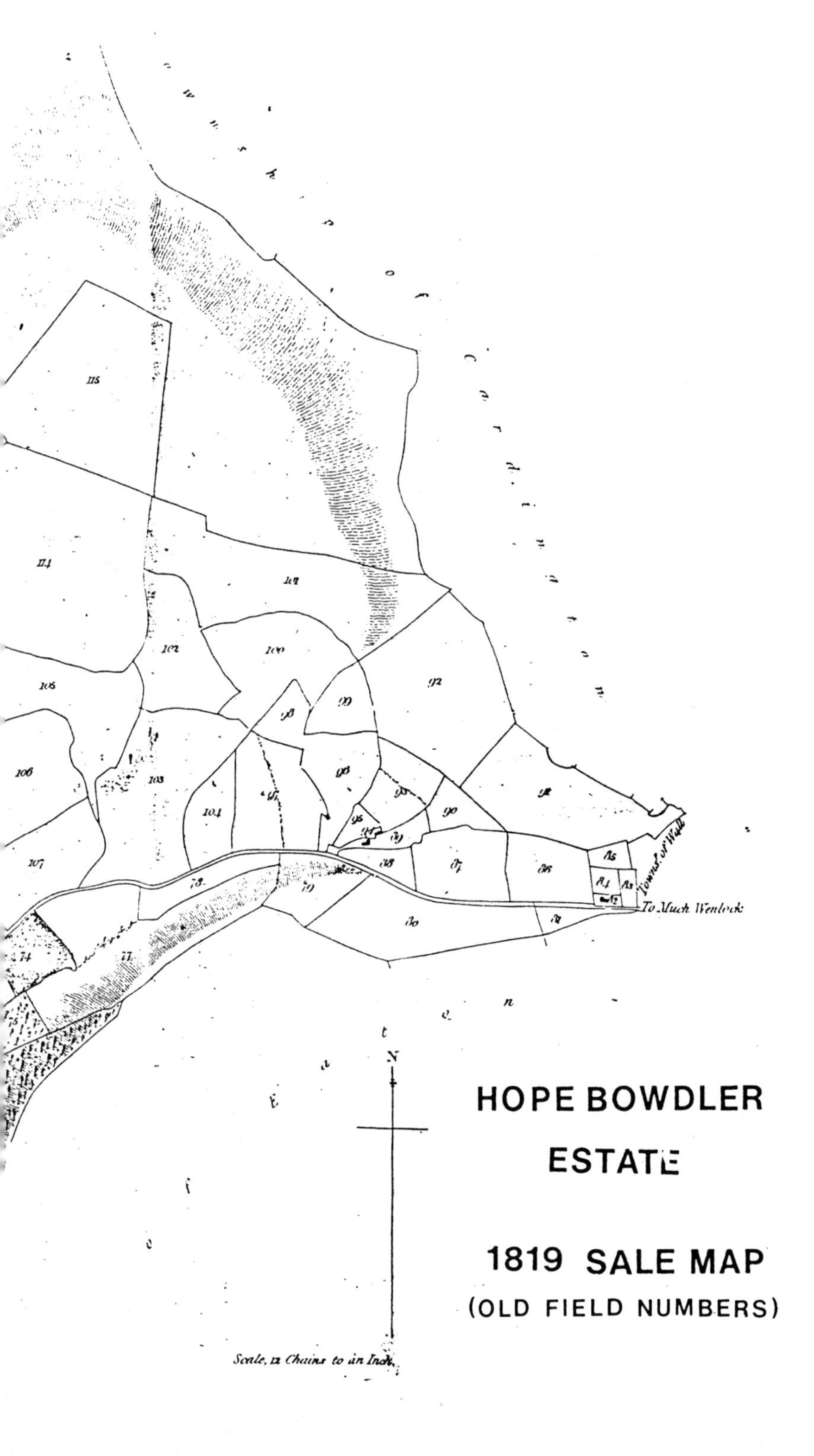

HOPE BOWDLER ESTATE

1819 SALE MAP

(OLD FIELD NUMBERS)

old no	*Landowner*- R A Benson *Tenant* - William Adams Manor Farm	*Tithe* no	*a r p*	*Description*
70/1	House, buildings, fold, garden	83	1 2 38	
72	Stack Yard	82	3 6	
73/4	Great Meadow	81	10 2 12	Meadow
77	Plantation	80	10 2 35	Plantation
77	Middle Yells	73	4 1 0	Pasture
75	Little Yells	78	3 1 0	Arable
77	Upper Yells	70	6 1 30	Pasture
77	The Yells	74	4 2 0	Pasture
78	The Long Yells	69	3 1 15	Pasture
79	The Rickyard Field	67	5 1 27	Meadow
80	Large Enclosure	61	11 2 8	Arable
60	Hollow Meadow	105	6 1 14	Meadow
62	The Close	104	2 28	Meadow
59	Mead Furlong	117	5 3 2	Arable
103	Tinkers Ground	75	17 0 32	Pasture
104	Brickkiln Field	68a	4 3 24	Arable
102	Yew Tree Field	43	9 0 19	Arable
70	Garden adjoining Hall	84	27	Fold
42	Mill Hill Meadow	140	3 1 34	Arable
41	Dunstall Meadow	141	3 0 2	Meadow
40	Cow Pasture	139	5 0 5	Pasture
39	The Buttresses	138	7 3 7	Arable
38	The Buttresses	143	4 0 15	Arable
37	Big Low Field	142	7 0 4	Arable
35/6	Little Low Field	144	5 3 0	Arable
34	Quarry Leasow	145	5 3 13	Arable
	Annual Tithe due - £25-8-6		148 2 37	
	Landowner - R A Benson *Tenant* - William Adams Woodgate Cottage			
94	House, Buildings, Garden	65	17	
95	Little Meadow	64	2 3 33	Pasture
93	Part of Crofts	49	2 1 0	Arable
96	Cow Pasture & Garden	66	5 3 3	Pasture
97	Near Brick Kiln Field	68	7 3 28	Pasture
99	Quarry Leasow	47	3 1 26	Arable
100	Little Broomy Field	45	5 0 0	Arable
100	Big Broomy Field	44	7 3 31	Arable
92	Upper Shed Pasture	46	8 1 0	Pasture
92	Lower Shed Pasture	48	10 2 25	Arable
88	Barn Yard	62	1 2 33	Meadow
89	Barn and Yard	63	1 2 11	Pasture
90	Small Pipe Field	51	2 0 13	Pasture
87	Big Meadow	60	6 1 14	Meadow
			65 3 34	
	Share of Sheep Walk		110 0 0	
	Annual Tithe due - £11-11-6		175 3 34	

old no	Landowner - R A Benson Tenant - John Bluck Upper House Farm	Tithe no	a	r	p	Description
124	House, Bldgs, Fold & Garden	88a		1	27	
125	Banky Close	88		3	26	Pasture
128	Harpers Close	92	3	0	31	Pasture
133	Road	92a		1	5	
134	The Patches	89	6	1	11	Arable
135	Banky Meadow	91	3	3	37	Meadow
136	Cote Ground	31	4	3	0	Arable
136	Part of Cote Ground	90	6	3	13	Pasture
137	Hanging Meadow	30	3	1	17	Pasture
123	House Meadow	88b	7	0	15	Meadow
122	Rackles	88c	3	1	30	Arable
120	Cockshut Field	88d	7	1	14	Pasture
121	Wall Leasow	88e	3	0	28	Arable
111	Brantail	88f	4	2	27	Arable
110	Light Spout	88g	3	2	21	Arable
119	Flat Meadow	34	4	1	31	Arable
118	Ferny Ley	32	8	1	4	Arable
117	Lady Field Leasow	33	8	3	1	Arable
116	Old House Leasow	35	11	0	9	Arable
113	Bird Laurel	36	8	0	19	Pasture
112	Robins Rough	37	8	2	3	Pasture
109	How Beach	38	6	2	24	Pasture
			115	0	33	
	Share of Sheep Walk		67	0	0	
	Annual Tithe due - £21-5-0		182	0	33	
	Landowner - R A Benson Tenant - John Collins					
127	House, Buildings, Garden	86		1	7	
126	Orchard	87		2	22	Pasture
107	Yew Tree Meadow	76	8	2	23	Meadow
106	Little Mint	39	11	1	1	Arable
105	Gorsty Bank	41	5	3	33	Pasture
105	Part of Gorsty Bank	42	5	2	0	Arable
105	Part of Gorsty Bank	40	4	2	0	Arable
108	Road	38a		2	33	
			37	1	39	
	Share of Sheep Walk		18	0	0	
	Annual Tithe due - £5-8-0		55	1	39	

old no	*Landowner* - R A Benson *Tenant* - Thomas Oakley Lower Farm	*Tithe* no	*a*	*r*	*p*	*Description*
55	House, Buildings, Garden	101		3	4	
54	Close	119		1	19	Pasture
57	Hemp Yard	118		2	22	Meadow
58	Evans Meadow	121	7	2	36	Meadow
26	Bull Meadow	135	7	1	24	Meadow
25	Bull Piece	134	5	0	33	Arable
24	The Moors	148	4	2	19	Arable
23	The Moors	147	6	0	34	Arable
23	The Moors	157	7	2	0	Pasture
22	Road	157a		3	5	
20	Cowpasture	149	1	3	14	Pasture
19	Cow Leasow	125	5	3	22	Arable
21	Little Cow Leasow	133	2	1	30	Pasture
17/8	The Furlong	126	9	0	3	Arable
16	Hanging Way	29	10	0	28	Arable
15	Hope	28	5	3	2	Arable
8	Hazler Close	131	9	1	30	Arable
	Hazler Barn	130				
7	Chickery Field	132	10	1	9	Arable
6	Little Chickery Field	151	4	2	23	Arable
4	Lower Cainall	156	5	1	26	Arable
3	Cainall	152	8	0	39	Arable
1	Broomy Leasow	155	9	3	36	Arable
140	Turnpike Meadow	24	5	2	36	Meadow
139	Hopes Corner	19	7	3	22	Arable
139	Whistlement	25	8	2	0	Arable
139	Whistlement	26	5	2	14	Pasture
138	Upper Hanging Meadow	27	5	1	14	Meadow
142	Road	19a		1	30	
9	Hazler Broom	127	9	2	9	Arable
10	Inclosure from Hazler	129	10	1	23	Arable
10	Inclosure from Hazler	153	9	1	3	Arable
11	Inclosure from Hazler	128	7	2	15	Pasture
29	Towns-end	123	2	1	25	Pasture
28	Towns-end	122	2	0	17	
32	Broad Beach	135a	2	1	16	
	Buildings &c	130	2	0	0	
			213	1	32	
	Share of Sheep Walk		110	0	0	
	Annual Tithe due - £38-2-0		313	1	32	

old no	*Landowner* - R A Benson *Tenant* - Himself Hope Bowdler Hill	*Tithe No* 1	*a r p* 323 2 18	*Description*
	Landowner - R A Benson *Tenant* - Thomas Jones Cwm Farm			
154	House, buildings, garden	11	3 15	
155	Plantation	12	1 35	Plantation
156	,,	10	1 0 15	,,
157	Orchard	8	2 32	Pasture
158	Barn Yard	9	3 3 19	,,
159	Plantation	7	1 2 32	Plantation
160	The Meadow	6	8 3 17	Meadow
161	Aldery Meadow	5	2 3 21	Pasture
162	Lower Knowles	4	3 0 2	Arable
163	Upper Knowles	2	8 0 34	Pasture
163	Middle Knowles	3	6 1 0	Arable
164	Barley Butts	2a	5 1 0	Pasture
151	Turnpike Field	18	3 3 5	Arable
151	Near Turnpike Field	17	2 3 0	Arable
150	Road	16	1 1 28	
152	Middle Field	14	3 3 35	Arable
153	Garden Field	13	5 0 1	Pasture
			57 2 29	
	Share of Sheep Walk		21 0 0	
	Annual Tithe due - £4-14-0		78 2 29	
	Landowner - R A Benson *Tenant* - Samuel Bowen			
141	Cottage & Garden	15	3 0	
	Landowner - R A Benson *Tenant* - Bezaleel Croxton			
45	Part of Pool	110	27	Water
44	Walkers Close	111	29	Meadow
47	Part of Quarry Field	107	2 3 23	Pasture
47	Little Meadow	108	1 0 32	Arable
48	Pool Meadow	116	4 0 21	
	Annual Tithe due - £1-10-0		9 1 12	
	Landowner - R A Benson *Tenant* - John Sankey			
12	Broomy Field	22	2 0 32	Pasture
14	Little Hope	23	3 28	Pasture
	Annual Tithe due - 8s 0d		3 0 20	

old no	Landowner - R A Benson Tenant - John Morgan	Tithe No	a r p	Description
13	Toll House	20	2	
13	Garden	21	14	
			16	
	Landowner - R A Benson *Tenant* - John Sankey Woodgate Farm			
83	The Meadow	55	2 1 28	Meadow
86	Cabbage Field	58	3 1 27	Arable
86	Part of Cabbage Field	59	2 0 0	Pasture
91	Far Gill Moor	52	5 0 0	,,
91	Middle Gill Moor	53	4 2 0	,,
91	Lower Gill Moor	54	3 1 12	,,
81	Little Enclosure	57	1 0 25	Meadow
	Annual Tithe due - £3		21 3 12	
	Landowner - R A Benson *Tenant* - Mathew Hall, Woodgate			
82	Cottage & Garden	56	31	
	Landowner - R A Benson *Tenant* - Thomas Mawn, Woodgate			
82	Cottage & Garden	56a	31	
	Landowner - R A Benson *Tenant* - William Williams			
68/9	House & Garden	85	1 12	
	Landowner - R A Benson *Tenant* - Rowland Galliers			
63	House & Garden	103	29	
	Wheelwrights Shop & Garden	99	1 18	
			2 7	
	Landowner - R A Benson *Tenant* - Samuel Williams			
	House & Garden	112	19	
	Landowner - R A Benson *Tenant* - James Sheffield			
	Garden	115	1 1	

old no	*Landowner* - R A Benson *Tenant* - John Wilding	Tithe no	a r p	Description
76	Part of Upper Mount Flirt Annual Tithe due - 6s 0d	71	1 2 22	
	Landowner - R A Benson *Tenant* - Robert Everall			
76	Part of Mount Flirt	72	1 3 36	Arable
76	Part of field nr Upper Haywood	79	1 2 16	,,
	Part of field nr Upper Haywood	106	1 2 25	,,
	Annual Tithe due - £1		5 0 37	
	Landowner - John Broom *Tenant* - John Griffiths			
43	House & Garden	113	18	
	Landowner - John Broom *Tenant* - James Sheffield			
43	House & Garden	114	10	
	Landowner - Bezaleel Croxton *Tenant* - himself			
65	House, buildings, garden	100	29	
66pt	Garden	102a	2	
67	Smithy	98	2	
			33	
	Landowner - Rev G W Marsh (Glebe) *Tenant* - himself			
129	Rectory House & Lawn	96	3 12	
129	Garden	95	1 4	
129	Buildings & Yard	97	1 17	
56	Church & Churchyard	102	2 0	
			1 3 33	

	Landowner - Rev G W Marsh (Glebe) *Tenant* - John Bluck			
130	Pool Meadow	94	1 1 27	Meadow
131	Banky Meadow	93	1 3 20	,,
	Little Pike	124	1 0 0	Arable
30	Far Townsend Field	136	2 3 28	Meadow
31	Near Townsend Field	137	3 0 2	,,
33	Broad Brotch	146	2 1 3	Arable
5	Slandy Well	150	1 2 0	,,
2	Hazler Field	154	4 0 26	,,
	Cote Meadow	77	5 0 35	Meadow
	Upper Dol	221	8 2 12	Arable
	Lower Dol	222	11 3 21	,,
	Annual Tithe due - £8		45 3 14	
	Landowner - Rev G W Marsh *Tenant* - Thomas Oakley			
53	Little Close	120	22	
	Landowner - Shrewsbury Borough Charities Trust *Tenant* - Bezaleel Croxton			
49	Hope Bowdler Close	109	3 34	
	Annual Tithe due - 3s 6d			
Landowner - Shrewsbury Borough Charities Trust *Tenant* - Thomas Rogers Upper Farm, Chelmick				
House, buildings, fold, yard		241	2 24	
Wainhouse Close		242	1 1 19	Pasture
Brandy Furlong		226	8 1 4	Arable
Sideland Cold Hill		213	9 2 20	Pasture
Little Cold Hill		223	3 2 4	Arable
Little ,, ,,		214	7 3 20	,,
Dry Hill		215	3 0 8	,,
Quarry Leasow		218	6 0 10	,,
Near Cross Field		219	6 3 17	,,
Far ,, ,,		220	6 1 19	Pasture
Ditch Cop		243	3 1 27	Arable
Vetch Stubble		246	6 2 1	,,
Meadow before the House		248	5 2 27	,,
Further Yard		247	3 3 27	Arable
Upper Hatch		263	5 1 0	,,
Hatch Meadow		252	4 1 33	Meadow

	Tithe no	a r p	Description
Cowpasture with rough	234	9 1 36	Pasture
The Pikes	253	7 2 25	Arable
Hill Headland	236	4 0 34	,,
Goodlong Meadow	232	5 1 16	Meadow
Turnip Leasow	197	3 2 1	Arable
Lower ,,	230	3 1 30	,,
Upper Mill Leasow	201	3 0 13	,,
Lower Mill Leasow	202	2 2 15	,,
Soudley Spawns	183	3 21	Meadow
Backside	227	6 0 4	Arable
Annual Tithe due - £23-18-0		129 0 15	
Landowner - Thomas Dunne *Tenant* - Thomas Wilding Ragdon Farm & Chelmick			
House, buildings, garden, fold	291	2 0 0	
Yard Head	288	10 0 5	Pasture
Little Moors	287	3 3 6	Arable
Barn Yard	286	7 2 6	,,
Rye Grass Piece	282	5 2 32	Pasture
Sideland Meadow	283	6 1 11	Meadow
Gorsty Bank	299	3 0 6	Pasture
Briery Leasow	301	11 0 6	Meadow
Tinkers Meadow	302	13 0 8	,,
Pool Leasow	300	9 0 12	Arable
Near Ditch Field	296	8 3 23	,,
Butchers Leasow	293	10 2 38	,,
House, garden, barn, yard	249	1 16	
Broad Meadow	238	6 0 16	Meadow
Pike ,,	251	2 1 27	Arable
The Spawns	195	1 1 11	,,
Knowle Stock	205	4 1 1	,,
The Brotches	261	5 3 26	,,
Far Brotches	262	7 1 24	Pasture
Lower ,,	258	4 0 23	Arable
Little ,,	260	2 36	Pasture
Broad Leasow	264	8 2 10	Arable
Further ,,	265	4 0 12	,,
Brand Yard	266	2 3 16	,,
Backside Leasow	267	6 1 10	Pasture
Pike Furlong	285	7 2 30	,,
Road	286a	1 0 32	
Garden	250	38	
Further Ditchfield	296a	6 1 10	Arable
Annual Tithe due - £29		161 0 11	

	Tithe no	a r p	Description
Landowner - Thomas Dunne *Tenant* - himself			
Brotch Coppice	259	3 3 24	Coppice
Annual Tithe due - 4s 0d			
Landowner - John P Stanier *Tenant* - Martha Haynes Ragdon Manor Farm			
House, buildings, garden, fold	279	1 1 2	
Colliers Yard	292	3 2 17	Pasture
Near Old Field	290	5 0 5	Arable
The Old Yard	289	5 1 33	,,
Part of Upper Moor	297	9 3 24	Pasture
Lower Moor	298	10 2 20	,,
Garden Meadow	281	9 1 21	Meadow
Stackyard ,,	280	5 2 1	,,
Barn Yard	277	6 0 0	Pasture
Meadow	269	9 0 15	,,
Cowpasture	270	5 2 27	Arable
Churchyard Meadow	271	3 0 28	Meadow
Near Dales	276	5 2 15	Arable
Further ,,	272	5 3 19	,,
Quarry Leasow	217	3 0 7	,,
Further Marrols	295	8 3 30	,,
Near ,,	294	10 3 28	,,
Hill Field	274	10 1 12	,,
Piece above the road	275	7 1 20	,,
Oxpasture	273	10 0 0	,,
Old Shop Leasow	216	7 3 3	,,
Further Ditch	244	5 2 24	,,
The Ditch Cop	245	7 1 11	,,
Rag Batch	284	8 1 23	Pasture
The Hearne	268	9 3 37	,,
Road	278	1 27	
Annual Tithe due - £34-4-0		178 1 9	
Landowner - Honble Nugent *Tenant* - Robert Haynes Chelmick Manor Farm			
House, buildings, garden, fold	240	1 0 8	
Orchard	239	1 12	
Barn Yard	231	5 0 20	Meadow
Hill Headlands	237	3 7	Arable
,, ,,	235	1 2 30	,,
The Big Saplings	233	9 1 17	,,
The Lower ,,	193	10 3 15	,,

	Tithe no	a r p	Description
Upper Little Saplings	194	4 1 23	,,
Lower Chelmick Meadow	196	7 0 26	Meadow
Big Cote Leasow	198	5 3 16	Arable
Upper Chelmick Meadow	199	8 0 27	Meadow
Little Cote Leasow	200	3 1 14	Arable
Backside Field	229	5 0 34	,,
Little Backside Field	228	4 2 5	,,
Road	206	20	
The Sleeve	207	8 1 36	Pasture
Sheep Pasture	208	10 0 4	,,
Lower Stockings	209	7 1 1	,,
The Stocking	210	11 0 28	,,
Spring Piece	211	4 0 20	,,
Spring Copy	212	3 0 24	Wood
Upper Feg Field	224	6 1 5	Arable
Lower ,, ,,	225	5 0 27	,,
Burgess Bank	158	3 3 33	Pasture
Pool	162	1 16	Water
,,	165	1 5	,,
The Guinea Meadow	203	2 22	Meadow
Annual Tithe due - £22-16-0		128 3 15	
Landowner - Honble Nugent *Tenant* - Thomas Griffiths			
Patch	172	2 5	Arable
The Far Meadow	179	1 1 0	Meadow
Near ,,	181	1 1 39	,,
Little ,,	184	2 15	,,
Cottage & Garden	185	1 2	
Annual Tithe due - 14s 0d		4 0 21	
Landowner - Honble Nugent *Tenant* - Edward Cadwallader			
Cottage & Garden	174	2 23	
Landowner - Honble Nugent *Tenant* - Richard Cadwallader			
House & Garden	175	3 24	
Landowner - Honble Nugent *Tenant* - Ann Richards			
The Slang	176	1 20	Arable
Sideland Piece	177	2 0 14	,,
House & Garden	186	1 0	
The Meadow	187	1 5	Meadow
Lower Meadow	188	2 14	,,
Annual Tithe due - 12s 0d		3 2 13	

	Tithe no	a r p	Description
Landowner - Honble Nugent *Tenant* - Edward Mason			
Garden	178	1 9	Arable
,,	180	1 3	,,
House & Garden	189	1 35	
Croft	190	2 14	,,
Annual Tithe due - 5s 0d		1 2 21	
Landowner - Honble Nugent *Tenant* - William Harley			
Orchard	159	1 14	Pasture
House, buildings, garden	160	14	
Little Meadow	161	36	
Garden	163	14	
Piece over the Pool	164	1 36	Pasture
Banky Piece	204	3 23	Arable
The Meadow	204a	34	Meadow
Quarry Piece	167	1 0 10	Pasture
Annual Tithe due - 16s 0d		3 1 21	
Landowner - Mrs Stackhouse *Tenant* - William Wall			
The Spawns	192	11 0 35	Pasture
The Pikes	254	4 0 31	Arable
The old lands	255	7 3 37	Pasture
,, ,, ,,	256	1 12	,,
The Copy Piece	257	3 3 24	Arable
Part of Common Spawns	191	1 1 13	Pasture
The Little Spawns	182	3 17	Meadow
Annual Tithe due - £4-5-0		29 3 9	
Landowner - Honble Nugent *Tenant* - John Griffiths			
House, buildings, garden, quarry	166	3 11	
Garden	168	1 16	Arable
Banky Piece	170	3 15	,,
Slang	169	1 33	,,
Annual Tithe due - 7s 0d		2 1 35	
Landowner - Honble Nugent *Tenant* - Thomas Humphries			
House & Garden	171	2 23	
Slang	173	21	
		3 4	

INDEX - 18-20 Century Names

75.
8.9.87
Durkers